EFFECTIVENESS IN WRITING

By Helen Driver, Natascha Gast,
and Susan Lowman-Thomas

Edited by Kim Jacobs

American Public University System ePress

2012

Revised 2015

Authors: Helen Driver, Natascha Gast, and Susan Lowman-Thomas
Content Editor: Kimberly Jacobs
Acquisitions Editor: Judith Novak
Production Editor: Molly Fischer
Editor in Chief: Fred Stielow

Cover Illustration: Jessica Radlich,
American Public University System Visual Arts

Printed in the United States of America
This text was compiled in Charles Town, West Virginia by the APUS ePress.

This book uses constantly changing technologies, and is frequently updated to ensure links are accessible.

ISBNs: 978-1-937381-07-3 (e-book)
978-1-937381-13-4 (print book)

American Public University System ePress
111 West Congress Street
Charles Town, WV 25414

www.apus.edu http://apus.campusguides.com/APUS_ePress

ABOUT THE PRINT EDITION OF THIS BOOK

This textbook was created first and foremost to be an interactive e-book.

Consequently, some of the interactivity is lost in the printed version. In this version,

hyperlinks and URLs are underlined and shown in gray. Visit

http://ezproxy.apus.edu/login?url=http://ebooks.apus.edu/ENGL102/ENGL102_Jan2014_

ebook.pdf and log in to access the e-book version.

TABLE OF CONTENTS

CHAPTER 1: INTRODUCTION TO ENGLISH 102 - EFFECTIVENESS IN WRITING

INTRODUCTION

Welcome to English 102 – Effectiveness in Writing. In this course, you will learn how to evaluate and write argumentative essays. You will also continue to develop and strengthen your knowledge of research and citation.

Most of you have taken English 101. In that course, you were introduced to academic writing, research, and citation. You also received refreshers in grammar and paragraphing. This course will expand upon your academic writing and research abilities and help you move to writing persuasive researched essays. These essays will be modeled after argumentative styles: the Toulmin, the Rogerian, and the middle-ground argumentative styles specifically. You will also learn how to locate academic sources to help you prove your case in these essays, and you will learn how to approach these academic sources in a critical way – observing when these works use the modes of persuasion correctly and when certain sources make mistakes. Finally, you will discover how reading critically and effectively persuading an audience can help you achieve your educational and career goals. This is a lot to cover. Don't worry, though! We have an entire semester to learn this information.

During this first section of the course, you will be introduced to persuasion, argumentation, developing and supporting a claim, the argumentative structure, and argumentative fallacies. All of these topics will be expanded later in this course. You will also refresh your knowledge of the MLA format and learn how evaluating your current writing style could help strengthen your writing abilities.

INTRODUCTION TO PERSUASIVE ARGUMENTS

This course focuses upon the art of persuasion and argumentation. In this course, both elements are connected. In order to persuade an audience, one must have an effective argument. When we use persuasion in this course, we will think of persuasion as the act of convincing another person or group of a belief using rational means.

Persuasion is sometimes thought of as being similar to propaganda – where one group attempts to influence people through biased, often incorrect, information in order to benefit that first group.

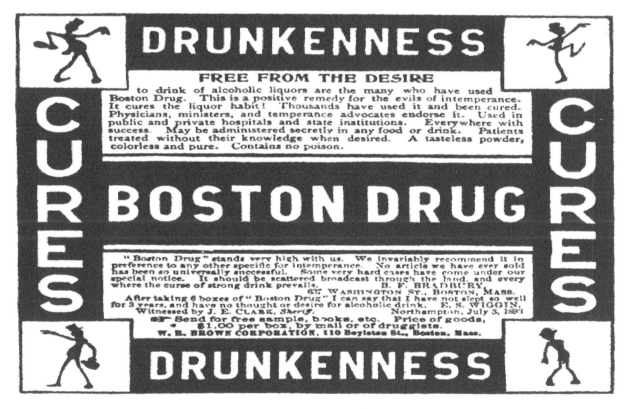

Fig. 1.1 A patent medicine advertisement from the W.E. Brown Corporation of Boston, Massachusetts, circa 1893. The advertisement shows caricatures of drunken men holding bottles and contains the text, "BOSTON DRUG CURES DRUNKENESS. Free from the desire to drink alcoholic liquors are the many who have used Boston Drug. This is a positive remedy for the evils of intemperance. It cures the liquor habit! Thousands have used it and been cured..." Two customer testimonials are also given.

An example of this sort of persuasive propaganda can be seen above in Figure 1.1:

This advertisement from 1893 claims to sell a drug that cures users from desiring alcohol. The advertisement gives vague statistics: "Thousands have used it and been cured." However, this advertisement gives no specific 'facts' and no specific research as to how these studies occurred. Although the drug apparently contains "no poison," is this drug doctor approved? There are two quotations, vaguely showing some sort of authority, but as we know, the author of the advertisement could have easily created the quotations. Because there is no specific evidence, this advertisement is biased. It is not *convincing another person or group of a belief using rational means*. Therefore, this sort of persuasive propaganda is not the type of persuasive argumentation we will use in this course. We will learn how to recognize this sort of propaganda and how to avoid using these as sources for our arguments.

Next is an example of an advertisement that convinces viewers of a belief using rational means (see Fig. 1.2):

Fig. 1.2: A red, white, and blue graphic shows a boy with a bandaged head and eye. The text reads "Dept. of Health, New York City. Be Wise: Don't Play with Firecrackers."

Like the former advertisement, this advertisement attempts to influence the viewer. However, unlike the drug advertisement, this advertisement does not falsify information. Instead, the clear image of a young boy who has experienced an eye injury emotionally affects the viewer. This image is based on reason - most realize that this sort of injury can easily occur when children play with firecrackers. Therefore, this advertisement utilizes a rational, persuasive method to influence viewers.

If persuasion is the act of convincing another person or group of a belief using rational means, persuasive argumentation, then, occurs when one uses rational means to convince a group of a belief that contains a counterclaim. Oftentimes, argumentation is viewed as a competition between two sides where one side wins and the other loses. Much of media perpetuates this myth about argumentation, portraying two or more people on opposite sides of the spectrum, emotionally throwing jabs at each other. Each side poised to *win* the argumentative competition through any means necessary.

Fig. 1.3 An oil painting entitled *Argument Over a Card Game* by Dutch painter Jan Steen (1626-1679). A woman and child restrain a man from lunging toward a seated man pointing a knife. Onlookers laugh at the scene. A backgammon board, an overturned pitcher, and scattered cards lay on the ground. Oil on canvas, 90 x 119 cm, Staatliche Museen, Berlin. http://commons.wikimedia.org/wiki/File:Steen_Argument_over_a_Card_Game.jpg{{PD-US}} – published in the US before 1923 and public domain in the U.S.

This competitive method of argumentation can be seen throughout written history. As an example, please view the following YouTube clip: <u>Short Clip from *The Taming of the Shrew* performed on stage in 1976 by the unique American Conservatory Theater in San Francisco</u>. A <u>transcript</u> of this clip can be found at the end of this lesson. The clip from the play *The Taming of the Shrew,* written by William Shakespeare, shows the competitive argument at its best. The two characters in the play are Petruchio, who searches for a wealthy wife, and Katharina, the unmarried daughter of a wealthy business owner. Although Petruchio knows that Katharina is an angry and temperamental young woman, he overlooks this flaw in order to gain access to her wealth. In the scene from the clip, Petruchio has set out to woo Katharina by sending complements her way. However, Petruchio soon learns that Katharina will not be easily persuaded through the usual compliments, so he decides instead to try sparring verbally with her. Unfortunately, instead of persuading Katharina to be his wife, the discussion begins to take a hostile turn and Petruchio becomes angry. Through this he forgets his goal: wooing the beautiful Katharina. Instead, he focuses on winning the argument and not achieving his purpose. Instead of romantically wooing her, he insults her.

We have seen these sorts of arguments before in movies, in literature, and life. Two characters boldly face each other flying witty statements back and forth – in a circular fashion. Although the effect is enjoyable for the audience to witness, nothing becomes accomplished through these sorts of discussions, and these types of heated verbal bantering back and forth are simply cathartic venting. Instead, persuasive argumentation focuses more on convincing someone to agree with one side of an issue, rather than verbal competition. The argument is a means to an end. One should avoid succumbing to emotion and the temptation to make this argument an end in and of itself.

In this course, you will learn how to effectively persuade an audience to agree with a claim: a specific stance on a topic. That is, in this course, you write persuasive arguments. With this sort of argumentation, the person creating the argument must take the audience into consideration and decide what will win over that audience. The goal, then, in persuasive argumentation is not to persuade the audience through exaggerated information or to competitively win by any means necessary. The goal in persuasive argumentation is to persuade the audience to agree with your claim about an issue.

An example of this sort of persuasive argument is illustrated in Mark Twain's novel *Tom Sawyer*. In this novel, Tom Sawyer exhibits a strong persuasive ability. You probably are familiar with the fence painting scene in Chapter Two. However, to refresh your memory, please read that section from *Tom Sawyer* located at the end of this lesson.

In this scene, Tom Sawyer's aunt forces Tom to whitewash a fence as a punishment for skipping school. Tom desperately wants to do anything but whitewash the fence, but he soon realizes he cannot buy his way out of it. He then decides to persuade his friends to do the work for him. He knows that his friends will be convinced if they think that painting a fence is an exceptional event. Tom explains that in order to make a person "want" a thing, "it is only necessary to make the thing difficult to attain" (para. 27). Tom also knows that his friends will be further convinced to paint the fence if it appears to be enjoyable. He explains: "Work consists of whatever a body is *obliged* to do, and that Play consists of whatever a body is not obliged to do." Therefore, by showing his friend Ben how much fun painting a fence could be and explaining how painting this fence is a rare opportunity, Tom Sawyer persuades his audience, specifically his friend Ben, to paint that fence. In this way, Tom *wins* through a persuasive argument.

In this course, you will be considering and persuading your audience in a similar manner. Like Tom Sawyer, you will be using reason to persuade your audience to agree with issues that matter to you.

CHOOSING A TOPIC, MAKING A CLAIM ABOUT THAT TOPIC, AND COMBATING WRITER'S BLOCK

To persuasively and effectively argue a claim, it is helpful to care about that claim. Let's take a look at Twain's fence painting scene again. Note that Tom Sawyer clearly cares about persuading Ben: Tom "began to think of the fun he had planned for this day, and his sorrows multiplied. Soon the free boys would come tripping along on all sorts of delicious expeditions, and they would make a world of fun of him for having to work – the very thought of it burnt him like fire" (para. 3). This is an important component of argumentation. The argument should have some meaning to you. If the topic matters to you, then you will be more inclined to construct a strong argument.

Often students pick one of the old standbys – lowering the drinking age, capital punishment, and so on. These popular topics are tempting; however, most students do not have any personal experience with these topics. They have no immediate, personal stake in claims about these topics and, therefore, tend to write general overview arguments about these issues. When creating persuasive arguments, it is best to avoid abstract topics of this sort. Instead, think about the issues that matter to you in particular. For example, if you are a parent dealing with childcare issues, focus on that in your essays. If you are a history buff and truly enjoy reading about the Korean War, use that as a base for your opening research. If you are passionate about sports and fitness, find a claim about a topic within that field. Remember, if you care about the topic, that will come across to your reader in your argument.

Sometimes it takes a bit of work to decide upon a meaningful topic. If you are uncertain as to how to begin, start reading. Pick up some local newspapers and browse through the articles. This will provide you with basic knowledge about the latest issues that could potentially affect you personally. Local issues can often be a good place to start. Also, reading newspapers or watching television news can help you to obtain an idea of what sort of information is available for research. Consider branching out from the standard U.S. news sources and explore international sources like the *International Herald Tribune*, the *London Telegraph*, or the *British Broadcasting Corporation* (BBC), for instance. Another way to spark an idea for a claim is to briefly go through some of the discussion forums in your courses – what topics spark interesting discussions from your classmates? That may lead to a potential topic. Finally, if you are still drawing a blank, pull out a piece of paper and start jotting down concerns that you have personally. Perhaps one of these concerns would make for a strong persuasive essay.

Once you do have that 'spark' of an idea – continue to brainstorm. This is an important step because you need to control and specify your topic. Many brainstorming techniques have been discussed in English 101. However, if you would like to review these techniques, please try the following links: University of North Carolina at Chapel Hill's Writing Center - Brainstorming Techniques, The Writing Center at George Mason University, and The Writing Center at the University of Arkansas at Little Rock.

SUPPORTING AN ARGUMENT

In this course, you will learn how to effectively prove your chosen claim using the modes of persuasion: ethos (credibility), pathos (emotion), and logos (fact). We will delve deeper into the modes of persuasion as the course moves forward; however, just to give you an illustration on how these modes can effectively enhance an argument, think back to the

Tom Sawyer example. Tom attempts to use all three methods of support in his argument to Ben about the value in spending time whitewashing a fence. Tom illustrates credibility when he appears to be enchanted while he artistically paints the fence: "Tom swept his brush daintily back and forth – stepped back to note the effect – added a touch here and there – criticised the effect again" (para. 20). Tom uses both emotion (created jealousy in Ben) and fact (albeit exaggerated) when he stated: "I reckon there ain't one boy in a thousand, maybe two thousand, that can do it the way it's got to be done" (para. 21). Just like Tom uses the modes of persuasion to convince his audience, you will learn how to use the modes of persuasion to effectively convince your audience of a claim, as well.

ELEMENTS OF A PERSUASIVE ARGUMENT/ORGANIZATION

In order to persuade your audience, you not only need to prove your claim using the types of support as explained above, you need to know how to organize your support as well. In this course, you will learn several different argumentative methods of organization. However, these methods all contain similar concepts: warrants, backing, qualifiers, reservations, and rebuttals. Most arguments will contain a warrant. Warrants show how your support connects to your claim. Backing is often used to support a warrant. Qualifiers show how your claim, perhaps, is not universally true. Reservations explain the counterargument. Rebuttals are arguments against the counterclaim. All of these terms will be explained in more depth later in the course.

KNOW YOUR AUDIENCE

To effectively persuade an audience of your claim, you not only need to have strong, well-organized support, you also need to know your audience, since the purpose of persuasive argumentation is to persuade that audience to agree with your stance. Just as

Tom Sawyer considered what sort of information would convince Ben to paint that fence, you also need to consider what sort of information would persuade your audience.

Let's take a look at the Twain selection again. Tom Sawyer must convince Ben, a young boy around ten to twelve years old, of his argument. The modes of support, then, do not have to be as strong as they would for an educated adult. Even without knowing any of the argumentative fallacies (errors in argumentation) that will be taught later this semester, an educated adult can easily find flaws in Tom's argument. For example, Tom tells Ben that "I reckon there ain't one boy in a thousand, maybe two thousand, that can do it the way it's got to be done" (para. 21). An educated person would wonder where Tom discovered this information. Also, when Tom shows Ben all the fun to be had painting a fence, an educated audience would wonder if Tom's specific instance is universally true. In this course, you will learn how to persuade educated individuals. To convince educated people, you need to do more than point out personal opinions or make up facts. You must research a topic, for you need to cite facts that back up your claims. Unlike Tom, whose audience is a child, you will have to prove your argument through authoritative sources and in an academic manner.

RESEARCHING AN ARGUMENT

Finding effective sources can be tricky. However, in order to convince an audience, you must have support, and the strongest types of support can often be found in academic, authoritative sources. This course will teach you effective ways to research a topic. You will also discover where to locate academic sources and how to approach these sources in an active, critical way. Finally, you will learn how research can strengthen and specify your discussion.

NEGOTIATING THE OPPOSITION

Again, persuasive arguments use rational means to convince a group of a belief that contains a counterclaim. **When choosing a topic and deciding upon a claim, you must ensure that there is a counterclaim.** Otherwise, you turn your persuasive argument into an informative discussion. However, because there is a counterclaim, you must acknowledge it in your arguments. Ignoring the counterclaim could potentially lead your audience to believe that your argument is biased. In this course, you will learn why it is important to acknowledge the counter to your claim, and you will understand how to effectively approach a counterclaim. Developing effective and compelling rebuttals against counterclaims will also be discussed in this course.

INTRODUCTION TO ARGUMENTATIVE FALLACIES AND CRITICAL THINKING

When writing effectively and seeking sources, it is helpful to understand the traps that many fall into when creating an argument. These traps or argumentative fallacies should also be avoided in research. Becoming an active, critical thinker can help readers avoid these traps. When approaching an argument, you must move beyond simply understanding the content of that work. You need to think critically about the work – actively think about how and why that argument is formed. We will also delve deeper into the idea of reading critically later in this course.

Argumentative fallacies can be found in the two literature selections in this lesson. For example, in the section we read from Shakespeare's *The Taming of the Shrew,* we can see that Petruchio, in his quest for the lovely and spirited Katherina, insults her. This particular fallacy is called *ad hominem*. Many of us commit this fallacy in the heat of an argument, just like Petruchio. However, in written argumentation, you can easily discover and correct this sort of fallacy by stepping back and reviewing your work. Argumentative fallacies can also be found in the Tom Sawyer example. As explained earlier, Tom claims specific *facts* that aren't supported by solid research; he also tries to show a specific instance to be universally true. If Ben had thought critically about Tom's argument, he might have avoided giving in to Tom. However, being a young boy, Ben has an excuse to take the argument at face value. As a student of argumentation, you do not have that excuse.

EDITING, REVISING, AND MLA FORMATTING

After working so hard to find a strong topic, sort through academic research, and write a persuasive argument, you certainly do not want your essay to fall apart because you did not properly revise the content of your essay or edit your work for smaller grammatical errors. We will learn how to effectively manage proofreading and editing this semester. We will also learn how to cite sources effectively using the MLA citation style.

In this first lesson, you will learn how to correctly format an essay in MLA style. Please use this format in your writing assessment due this week and throughout the course. The parts of your assignment include a header, a heading, a title, the body of the essay, and when appropriate a works cited page. **Be sure to read the sample document below; it includes instructions in formatting.** Below is the sample format for the first letter:

In the header space, type Your Last Name and Page number

Your name

Your instructor

English 102

The date

The Title of Your Essay (Title your Letter)

This is a formatting sample. You need to make sure that you that you use a consistent font throughout your paper (most instructors prefer **12 point Times New Roman**). Note that **your last name and page number are at the top**. You need to insert them into your document header. Don't just type the last name and page number on every page. That is incorrect. If you have the latest version of Word, here's how: click on "Insert," "Page Number," "Top of the Page," and use the option "Plain Number 3." Then, click on the page number in the header. Place the curser to the left of the number, and type your name. The page numbers are not included in this formatting sample.

Notice that there are **no extra spaces in between each paragraph**. To space your paper correctly, do the following: click on "Paragraph." Make sure the spacing "Before" and "After" are both set to 0 pt. Also, make sure that the spacing is set to double. Click "OK." Do this before you type to **have the document set to double space automatically**. Or you can do this after you have completed your work – highlight the entire paper, and then set the spacing to double. Also, notice that each paragraph is tabbed in. Use the **"Tab" key to indent the first line of each new paragraph**.

The **entire paper's margins are set at 1 inch**. This means that there is one-inch of white space visible at the top, the bottom, the left, and the right of the text. To set these margins in the latest version of Word, click on the "Page Layout" tab. Click on "Margins." Choose "Normal" for which the top, bottom, left, and right margins measure "1 Inch."

If you are interested, please view this YouTube video which gives explicit details on how to format a paper MLA style: MLA Style Essay Format - Word Tutorial. This video was created by University of Maryland University College and is entitled "MLA Style Essay Format – Word Tutorial." It covers the information mentioned above. Please also click on this link for a helpful review of MLA documentation and formatting. This PowerPoint presentation gives an overview of formatting and information on MLA documentation.

EVALUATING YOUR WRITING STYLE

In this course, you will conduct written arguments. In order to create an effective written argument, you must have strong writing skills. To improve and strengthen these skills, it does help to evaluate the skills that you currently have. The first written assignment, the writing assessment, will help you do that. In it you will think critically about and discuss your current writing process and style. Not only will this assignment help you understand how you approach written work, It will give your instructor a general understanding of your writing style. After reading your assessment, your instructor will give you suggestions for improvement and will help you format your first essay.

CONCLUSION

This completes lesson one. Much was discussed in this first lesson. However, remember, you have an entire semester to master this information. Hopefully, you now have a strong understanding of what a persuasive argument is and a general feel for the layout of the course.

Questions to Consider

1. Think of a recent argument. Did you engage in the argument in order to win against

    or win over the other side?

2. Why is it important to consider your audience when creating a persuasive argument?

3. Why should your claims matter to you?

4. How might you use argumentation in your personal or professional lives?

Works Cited

"Brainstorming." *The Writing Center at University of North Carolina at Chapel Hill.* 2011.

Web. 15 Dec. 2011.

"Brainstorming Techniques." *The Writing Center at George Mason University.* 2009. Web. 15

Dec. 2011.

"Brainstorming Techniques." *The Writing Center at University of Arkansas at Little Rock.*

2009. Web. 15 Dec. 2011.

"File: Be Wise, Don't Play with Firecrackers." *Wikimedia Commons.* 31 Jan. 2010. Web. 15

Dec. 2011.

"File: Boston Drug for Drunkenness.png." *Wikimedia Commons.* 31 Jan. 2010. Web. 15 Dec.

2011.

"File: Steen Argument over a Card Game.jpg." *Wikimedia Commons.* 22 Mar. 2011. Web. 15

Dec. 2011.

"MLA Style Essay Format – Word Tutorial." *Online Posting.* YouTube, 10 Jan. 2011. Web. 23

May 2011.

"Taming of the Shrew – American Conservatory Theater." *Online Posting.* YouTube, 10 Jan.

2011. Web. 23 May 2011.

Twain, Mark. *Tom Sawyer. Project Gutenberg.* Project Gutenberg Literary Archive

Foundation, 2012. Web. 25 Jan. 2012.

LITERATURE TRANSCRIPTS
The Taming of the Shrew. Act 2, Scene 1, Lines 165-277

PETRUCHIO

I will attend her here,

And woo her with some spirit when she comes.

Say that she rail; why then I'll tell her plain

She sings as sweetly as a nightingale:

Say that she frown, I'll say she looks as clear

As morning roses newly wash'd with dew:

Say she be mute and will not speak a word;

Then I'll commend her volubility,

And say she uttereth piercing eloquence:

If she do bid me pack, I'll give her thanks,

As though she bid me stay by her a week:

If she deny to wed, I'll crave the day

When I shall ask the banns and when be married.

PETRUCHIO

Good morrow, Kate; for that's your name, I hear.

KATHARINA

Well have you heard, but something hard of hearing:

They call me Katharina that do talk of me.

PETRUCHIO

You lie, in faith; for you are call'd plain Kate,

And bonny Kate and sometimes Kate the curst;

But Kate, the prettiest Kate in Christendom

Kate of Kate Hall, my super-dainty Kate,

For dainties are all Kates, and therefore, Kate,

Take this of me, Kate of my consolation;

Hearing thy mildness praised in every town,

Thy virtues spoke of, and thy beauty sounded,

Yet not so deeply as to thee belongs,

Myself am moved to woo thee for my wife.

KATHARINA

Moved! in good time: let him that moved you hither

Remove you hence: I knew you at the first

You were a moveable.

PETRUCHIO

Why, what's a moveable?

KATHARINA

A join'd-stool.

PETRUCHIO

Thou hast hit it: come, sit on me.

KATHARINA

Asses are made to bear, and so are you.

PETRUCHIO

Women are made to bear, and so are you.

KATHARINA

No such jade as you, if me you mean.

PETRUCHIO

Alas! good Kate, I will not burden thee;

For, knowing thee to be but young and light--

KATHARINA

Too light for such a swain as you to catch;

And yet as heavy as my weight should be.

PETRUCHIO

Should be! should--buzz!

KATHARINA

Well ta'en, and like a buzzard.

PETRUCHIO

O slow-wing'd turtle! shall a buzzard take thee?

KATHARINA

Ay, for a turtle, as he takes a buzzard.

PETRUCHIO

Come, come, you wasp; I' faith, you are too angry.

KATHARINA

If I be waspish, best beware my sting.

PETRUCHIO

My remedy is then, to pluck it out.

KATHARINA

Ay, if the fool could find it where it lies,

PETRUCHIO

Who knows not where a wasp does

wear his sting? In his tail.

KATHARINA

In his tongue.

PETRUCHIO

Whose tongue?

KATHARINA

Yours, if you talk of tails: and so farewell.

PETRUCHIO

What, with my tongue in your tail? nay, come again,

Good Kate; I am a gentleman.

KATHARINA

That I'll try.

She strikes him

PETRUCHIO

I swear I'll cuff you, if you strike again.

KATHARINA

So may you lose your arms:

If you strike me, you are no gentleman;

And if no gentleman, why then no arms.

PETRUCHIO

A herald, Kate? O, put me in thy books!

KATHARINA

What is your crest? a coxcomb?

PETRUCHIO

A combless cock, so Kate will be my hen.

KATHARINA

No cock of mine; you crow too like a craven.

PETRUCHIO

Nay, come, Kate, come; you must not look so sour.

KATHARINA

It is my fashion, when I see a crab.

PETRUCHIO

Why, here's no crab; and therefore look not sour.

KATHARINA

There is, there is.

PETRUCHIO

Then show it me.

KATHARINA

Had I a glass, I would.

PETRUCHIO

What, you mean my face?

KATHARINA

Well aim'd of such a young one.

PETRUCHIO

Now, by Saint George, I am too young for you.

KATHARINA

Yet you are wither'd.

PETRUCHIO

'Tis with cares.

KATHARINA

I care not.

PETRUCHIO

Nay, hear you, Kate: in sooth you scape not so.

KATHARINA

I chafe you, if I tarry: let me go.

PETRUCHIO

No, not a whit: I find you passing gentle.

'Twas told me you were rough and coy and sullen,

And now I find report a very liar;

For thou are pleasant, gamesome, passing courteous,

But slow in speech, yet sweet as spring-time flowers:

Thou canst not frown, thou canst not look askance,

Nor bite the lip, as angry wenches will,

Nor hast thou pleasure to be cross in talk,

But thou with mildness entertain'st thy wooers,

With gentle conference, soft and affable.

Why does the world report that Kate doth limp?

O slanderous world! Kate like the hazel-twig

Is straight and slender and as brown in hue

As hazel nuts and sweeter than the kernels.

O, let me see thee walk: thou dost not halt.

KATHARINA

Go, fool, and whom thou keep'st command.

PETRUCHIO

Did ever Dian so become a grove

As Kate this chamber with her princely gait?

O, be thou Dian, and let her be Kate;

And then let Kate be chaste and Dian sportful!

KATHARINA

Where did you study all this goodly speech?

PETRUCHIO

It is extempore, from my mother-wit.

KATHARINA

A witty mother! witless else her son.

PETRUCHIO

Am I not wise?

KATHARINA

Yes; keep you warm.

PETRUCHIO

Marry, so I mean, sweet Katharina, in thy bed:

And therefore, setting all this chat aside,

Thus in plain terms: your father hath consented

That you shall be my wife; your dowry 'greed on;

And, Will you, nill you, I will marry you.

Now, Kate, I am a husband for your turn;

For, by this light, whereby I see thy beauty,

Thy beauty, that doth make me like thee well,

Thou must be married to no man but me;

For I am he am born to tame you Kate,

And bring you from a wild Kate to a Kate

Conformable as other household Kates.

Here comes your father: never make denial;

I must and will have Katharina to my wife.

From Mark Twain, *Tom Sawyer,* **Chapter Two, 1876.**

Saturday morning was come, and all the summer world was bright and fresh, and brimming with life. There was a song in every heart; and if the heart was young the music issued at the lips. There was cheer in every face and a spring in every step. The locust-trees were in bloom and the fragrance of the blossoms filled the air. Cardiff Hill, beyond the village and above it, was green with vegetation and it lay just far enough away to seem a Delectable Land, dreamy, reposeful, and inviting.

Tom appeared on the sidewalk with a bucket of whitewash and a long-handled brush. He surveyed the fence, and all gladness left him and a deep melancholy settled down upon his spirit. Thirty yards of board fence nine feet high. Life to him seemed hollow, and existence but a burden. Sighing, he dipped his brush and passed it along the topmost plank; repeated the operation; did it again; compared the insignificant whitewashed streak with the far-reaching continent of unwhitewashed fence, and sat down on a tree-box discouraged.

[...] He began to think of the fun he had planned for this day, and his sorrows multiplied. Soon the free boys would come tripping along on all sorts of delicious expeditions, and they would make a world of fun of him for having to work – the very thought of it burnt him like fire. He got out his worldly wealth and examined it – bits of toys, marbles, and trash; enough to buy an exchange of *work*, maybe, but not half enough to buy so much as half an hour of pure freedom. So he returned his straitened means to his pocket, and gave up the idea of trying to buy the boys. At this dark and hopeless moment an inspiration burst upon him! Nothing less than a great, magnificent inspiration.

He took up his brush and went tranquilly to work. Ben Rogers hove in sight presently – the very boy, of all boys, whose ridicule he had been dreading. Ben's gait was the hop-skip-and-jump – proof enough that his heart was light and his anticipations high. He was eating an apple, and giving a long, melodious whoop, at intervals, followed by a deep-toned ding-dong-dong, ding-dong-dong, for he was personating a steamboat. As he drew near, he slackened speed, took the middle of the street, leaned far over to star-board and rounded to ponderously and with laborious pomp and circumstance – for he was personating the Big Missouri, and considered himself to be drawing nine feet of water. He was boat and captain and engine-bells combined, so he had to imagine himself standing on his own hurricane-deck giving the orders and executing them:

"Stop her, sir! Ting-a-ling-ling!" The headway ran almost out, and he drew up slowly toward the sidewalk.

"Ship up to back! Ting-a-ling-ling!" His arms straightened and stiffened down his sides.

"Set her back on the stabboard! Ting-a-ling-ling! Chow! ch-chow-wow! Chow!" His right hand, meantime, describing stately circles – for it was representing a forty-foot wheel.

"Let her go back on the labboard! Ting-a-ling-ling! Chow-ch-chow-chow!" The left hand began to describe circles.

"Stop the stabboard! Ting-a-ling-ling! Stop the labboard! Come ahead on the stabboard! Stop her! Let your outside turn over slow! Ting-a-ling-ling! Chow-ow-ow! Get out that head-line! *Lively* now! Come – out with your spring-line – what're you about there! Take a turn round that stump with the bight of it! Stand by that stage, now – let her go! Done with the engines, sir! Ting-a-ling-ling! *Sh't! s'h't! sh't!*" (trying the gauge-cocks).

Tom went on whitewashing – paid no attention to the steamboat. Ben stared a moment and then said: "Hi- *yi* ! *You're* up a stump, ain't you!"

No answer. Tom surveyed his last touch with the eye of an artist, then he gave his brush another gentle sweep and surveyed the result, as before. Ben ranged up alongside of him. Tom's mouth watered for the apple, but he stuck to his work. Ben said:

"Hello, old chap, you got to work, hey?"

Tom wheeled suddenly and said: "Why, it's you, Ben! I warn't noticing."

"Say – *I'm* going in a-swimming, *I* am. Don't you wish you could? But of course you'd druther *work* – wouldn't you? Course you would!"

Tom contemplated the boy a bit, and said: "What do you call work?"

"Why, ain't *that* work?"

Tom resumed his whitewashing, and answered carelessly: "Well, maybe it is, and maybe it ain't. All I know, is, it suits Tom Sawyer."

"Oh come, now, you don't mean to let on that you *like* it?"

The brush continued to move. "Like it? Well, I don't see why I oughtn't to like it. Does a boy get a chance to whitewash a fence every day?"

That put the thing in a new light. Ben stopped nibbling his apple. Tom swept his brush daintily back and forth – stepped back to note the effect – added a touch here and there – criticised the effect again – Ben watching every move and getting more and more interested, more and more absorbed. Presently he said: "Say, Tom, let *me* whitewash a little."

Tom considered, was about to consent; but he altered his mind: "No – no – I reckon it wouldn't hardly do, Ben. You see, Aunt Polly's awful particular about this fence – right here on the street, you know – but if it was the back fence I wouldn't mind and *she* wouldn't. Yes, she's awful particular about this fence; it's got to be done very careful; I reckon there ain't one boy in a thousand, maybe two thousand, that can do it the way it's got to be done."

"No – is that so? Oh come, now – lemme, just try. Only just a little – I'd let *you*, if you was me, Tom."

"Ben, I'd like to, honest injun; but Aunt Polly – well, Jim wanted to do it, but she wouldn't let him; Sid wanted to do it, and she wouldn't let Sid. Now don't you see how I'm fixed? If you was to tackle this fence and anything was to happen to it – "

"Oh, shucks, I'll be just as careful. Now lemme try. Say – I'll give you the core of my apple."

"Well, here – No, Ben, now don't. I'm afeard – "

"I'll give you *all* of it!" Tom gave up the brush with reluctance in his face, but alacrity in his heart. And while the late steamer Big Missouri worked and sweated in the sun, the retired artist sat on a barrel in the shade close by, dangled his legs, munched his apple, and planned the slaughter of more innocents. There was no lack of material; boys happened along every little while; they came to jeer, but remained to whitewash. By the time Ben was fagged out, Tom had traded the next chance to Billy Fisher for a kite, in good repair; and when *he* played out, Johnny Miller bought in for a dead rat and a string to swing it with – and so on, and so on, hour after hour. And when the middle of the afternoon came, from being a poor poverty-stricken boy in the morning, Tom was literally rolling in wealth. He had besides the things before mentioned, twelve marbles,part of a jews-harp, a piece of blue bottle-glass to look through, a spool cannon, a key that wouldn't unlock anything, a fragment of chalk, a glass stopper of a decanter, a tin soldier, a couple of tadpoles, six fire-crackers, a kitten with only one eye, a brass door-knob, a dog-collar – but no dog – the handle of a knife, four pieces of orange-peel, and a dilapidated old window sash.

He had had a nice, good, idle time all the while – plenty of company – and the fence had three coats of whitewash on it! If he hadn't run out of whitewash he would have bankrupted every boy in the village.

Tom said to himself that it was not such a hollow world, after all. He had discovered a great law of human action, without knowing it – namely, that in order to make a man or a boy covet a thing, it is only necessary to make the thing difficult to attain. If he had been a great and wise philosopher, like the writer of this book, he would now have comprehended that Work consists of whatever a body is *obliged* to do, and that Play consists of whatever a body is not obliged to do. And this would help him to understand why constructing artificial flowers or performing on a tread-mill is work, while rolling ten-pins or climbing Mont Blanc is only amusement. There are wealthy gentlemen in England who drive four-horse passenger-coaches twenty or thirty miles on a daily line, in the summer, because the privilege costs them considerable money; but if they were offered wages for the service, that would turn it into work and then they would resign.

The boy mused awhile over the substantial change which had taken place in his worldly circumstances, and then wended toward headquarters to report.

Twain, Mark. *Tom Sawyer*. *Project Gutenberg*. Project Gutenberg Literary Archive
    Foundation, 2012. Web. 25 Jan 2012

Chapter 2: Developing Strong Research Techniques

Introduction

Research serves two key purposes: (1) for writers to discover more about the topic and (2) for writers to provide persuasive support for their ideas. This chapter will review ways to develop an effective research plan that allows you to find, evaluate, and use research appropriate for academic writing.

Types of Research

Preliminary Research

To learn more about a topic, start the research process with preliminary research, which provides background or a general overview of the topic. Go into this phase of research with an open mind. See what people debate. Examine the ideas on different sides of the issue. Preliminary research provides a better understanding of the agreed-upon issues related to the topic as well as the issues that the experts most often debate.

To find out what the experts typically debate, perhaps begin by researching the topic at one of these online debate databases:

- IDEA: International Debate Education Association

- ProCon.org

- OpposingViews

Such sources provide an overview of commonly debatable issues, which can help writers explore the many aspects of the debate.

During this preliminary stage of research, sources like encyclopedias (including Wikipedia) might be useful to gain general background about a topic, but ***these types of sources are only appropriate for preliminary research***. These sources provide background for the writer to understand the topic more fully. However, these sources, even credible encyclopedias, present facts only, and such facts will not need to be cited as secondary sources in the final written paper. Such resources are only appropriate as preliminary research.

Preliminary research is a place to start to gain a better understanding of the topic for yourself, the writer. Preliminary research should NOT be used as supporting research to prove ideas to an audience in the final written paper.

PRIMARY RESEARCH

Primary research involves direct observations or readings that are then analyzed or evaluated. For example, if you do an interview, experiment, or survey, then each interview, experiment or survey is primary research conducted directly by you. Such primary research is often called field research.

As another example, if you are analyzing something you've read, like a newspaper article or short story, then the article or short story is the primary research source. You are writing about that source (not using that source to support an argument about another topic). A politician's speech, for instance, might be a primary source if you are analyzing it to demonstrate the politician's flaws of reasoning or to argue in support of the policies presented by the speech.

SECONDARY RESEARCH

Secondary research is used to support ideas. For instance, if you are writing an argument about animal rights, then you might use statistics found in an article published by People for the Ethical Treatment of Animals as support for your argument. Those statistics from the article become evidence to support your argument and will need to be documented in the essay.

The next sections discuss ways to find secondary sources appropriate for academic writing.

DEVELOPING RESEARCH QUESTIONS

It's often a good strategy to think of the thesis statement of an essay as the answer to a question. For emphasis: *the thesis is not the question, but instead the thesis is the one-sentence answer to that question.* The essay proves that the thesis is the best answer to the question. For example, without knowing the position you might take on an issue, you may begin with the question, "Should there be laws prohibiting all types of graffiti?" The question is open-ended and allows for either a "yes" or "no" answer. To start the research, you might begin only with this question. (The final thesis of the paper will be the answer to the question with the essay proving why that is the best answer to the question.) This question is considered the primary research question. It is the one that the entire essay is attempting to answer.

Note: the primary research question for a persuasive argument essay should be one that reasonable people could answer differently. For instance, one reasonable person might write a persuasive essay arguing that graffiti should be banned while another reasonable person could write a persuasive essay arguing that graffiti should not be banned. In contrast, "What are the laws concerning graffiti?" would not be a good primary research question for an argument essay because the answer would be a report of the facts of what the current laws are (what the laws actually are cannot be debated). Recall from Chapter 1 that an argument must have a counterargument.

During the research and writing process, the primary research question might change. For instance, this primary research question about whether graffiti should be banned might change to "What should the law be concerning graffiti?" Thus, the thesis of the final essay would not be that there should or should not be a ban but instead the thesis might be that there should be a ban in certain areas or only a ban of certain types of graffiti.

After identifying a primary research question to get started, make a list of other questions that you will need to answer in order to answer your primary research question. These will be your secondary research questions. It's okay to add or remove questions to your list after you have begun researching.

There are four types of questions:

1. **Fact** – Questions of fact can be answered with data. Such questions:
    a. ask about things that can be measured or quantified in some way.
    b. ask about statistics, historical facts, or definitions.

2. **Value** – Questions of value focus on belief systems, societal norms, and the importance placed on an idea. Such questions:
    a. ask about the degree to which something is good or bad (ethical, moral, etc.).
    b. ask about priorities.

3. **Policy** – Questions of policy ask if something "should" be done. Such questions:
    a. ask about solutions to problems.
    b. ask about ideal situations.

4. **Prediction** – Questions of prediction ask about the future (to what degree or extent will something happen?). Such questions:

   a. ask about facts, events, values, or policies that might exist in the future.

   b. ask about what the impact of such future policies might be.

These secondary research questions are interconnected. For example, the following single research question leads to four additional related questions:

"How should society control graffiti?"

Fact: Where is graffiti found?

Value: Does graffiti harm property?

Policy: What should be done about graffiti?

Prediction: Will this policy stop graffiti in the future?

All four types of questions will be answered through your research. Remember, a good research question for an argument essay will be one that is a question of value, policy, or prediction (never a question of fact). However, fact questions will often need to be answered in research papers in order to support an answer to a question of value, policy, or prediction.

With such primary and secondary research questions in mind, the research process can become more focused by searching for answers to these questions rather than passively reading, and often becoming overwhelmed with, a lot of information from many sources.

IDENTIFYING KEYWORDS
With some research questions in mind, you can now begin to actually search for answers, starting with keywords present in your research questions. You might start with just

a few broad keywords to start your research. As you research more, additional keywords should emerge.

For example, during preliminary research on capital punishment, you might begin with just the words "capital punishment" in a simple web search engine. From that search, you might discover additional keywords relating to the debate, such as "retribution," "innocence," and "deterrence." You then might research such terms individually.

Try adding purpose keywords, too. For example, instead of searching only for "capital punishment," try searching for "pros," "cons," "debate," "argument," "support," "opposition," and other such terms that indicate that the search results should be focused on the debate around capital punishment.

Similarly, using synonyms for keywords can yield some good results. For example, instead of just "capital punishment," you might try "death penalty." Instead of "retribution" and "death penalty," you might try "vengeance" and "capital punishment."

Even using the file type as a keyword might return some very useful results! Try adding ".pdf" or ".doc" as keywords in a web search engine. Such file types, rather than general web pages, are more likely to be in a more professional publication format, making the chances more likely that the results will be scholarly or professional in nature than a general web page publication.

As you further explore a topic, you'll find that you might add or remove keywords in your search strategy or combine keywords differently based on the results you get. It takes some trial and error to get to the "good stuff." Thus, you might "mix and match" keywords to find good sources.

FINDING SOURCES

To find sources, just put your keywords into Google, right? Probably the most common way anyone does research nowadays is using an internet search engine, such as Google or one of these other popular ones:

- YAHOO!

- altavista

- bing

In addition, the following metacrawlers allow users to search multiple search engines from one site, providing the results from all the search engines in one place:

- mamma

- dogpile

- SurfWax

Such search engines can provide fast results, but are these results good? The results may be great for *preliminary research*, but sources found through these search engines must be evaluated very carefully to determine if they can be used as secondary sources appropriate for academic writing. In the next section we will discuss evaluating sources.

Google, in fact, recognized this need to filter academic sources from the many general web sources available online, so Google Scholar emerged. Google Scholar searches only for academic articles. However, many of these articles are not available for free access online, but you have access to them through your university's library.

Many free scholarly articles are accessible online, though. The following sites provide free full-text articles published in online scholarly journals:

- e-journals.org

- <u>DOAJ: Directory of Open Access Journals</u>

Also, some web portals are maintained by academics and professionals. These web portals provide subject directories and searchable databases of material already reviewed and confirmed to be academic in nature:

- <u>ipl2: Information You Can Trust</u>

- <u>The WWW Virtual Library</u>

- <u>questia: Trusted Online Research</u>

Of course, the most important academic web portal that you can use is the university's library. Your tuition has bought you access to many resources that are not freely available to the general public. The library buys subscriptions to many academic journals through services such as EBSCO Suite or ProQuest Suite. Each of these suites is a collection of many scholarly journals, most of which have full-text articles available for viewing online.

In addition to providing access to academic journals, the APUS Library provides access to online books, study guides, tutorials, and even "portals" that provide research sources specific to certain classes, all of which are wonderful options for academic research. To learn the most effective way to find academic research through the library, review the APUS Library's help pages on deep web searching. Please click on the following link: <u>APUS Deep Web Search Tips</u>. **Try starting your search with Summon from the APUS Library homepage** because this search engine covers nearly all of the articles, books, and other resources available through the online library Please click on the following link: <u>Summon</u>.

Finally, keep good records of the sites and resources you use for research. If you know of a site or section of the library that provided great information about a particular subject, bookmark it and use it again in the future. For instance, as you discover online journals and professional websites relevant to your major or career, keep track of them, so you can return to them again in the future.

Of course, it's also always a good idea to stay up-to-date on current events, tracking any breaking news on hot topics. This site provides a good place to start to link to the top 20 news sites online: netTOP20.com.

EVALUATING SOURCES

Using these many possible research avenues will lead to many possible sources. Researchers must quickly identify relevant and useful information from the vast amount of results found through online and library searches. When sifting through results, scan each article by reading the following:

1. Title

2. Abstract or summary (if any)

3. Headers of sections (if any)

4. Introductions and conclusions (first and last paragraphs)

5. First and last sentences of body paragraphs

These parts of an article can provide a good overview of the main ideas, allowing you to determine if the article is relevant to your research purposes.

Once you've determined that an article is relevant, ask yourself if it provides good support as well. For every ten relevant sources, maybe just one or two will actually end up in the final paper. Probably the easiest way to lose credibility with an audience is for the research sources to seem as if they were the first ones found through a Google search of the general web. Only the "best of the best" sources should be used as support in an academic essay.

What is the "best" type of source? The best source is one that will be persuasive for your target audience. When writing for academic purposes for an academic audience, the sources should be academic. The sources must not just be credible; they must be scholarly.

A credible source is one that can be reasonably trusted to be true, such as a news report published by a reputable newspaper. A scholarly source, in contrast, is one that is credible and targets an academic audience. A scholarly source is written by an expert in essay form and usually includes its own works cited or references section. For example, when it comes to medical topics, WebMD is a credible source, but *The New England Journal of Medicine* is a scholarly one. When it comes to international politics, *The New York Times* is a credible source, but *World Politics: A Quarterly Journal of International Relations* is a scholarly one.

For instance, let's say that you are writing an argument about how much funding should be provided for NASA's space program or the international space station. Obviously, NASA's website would be a credible source, but consider these two articles found on the NASA website:

- "Facts and Figures: International Space Station"

- "The Societal Impact of Space Flight"

The first is written by an expert (NASA itself), but it is just "facts and figures" about the international space station. It is not written as an essay and does not have its own works cited or references at the end. Its intended audience is the general public.

In contrast, the second is written by an expert (Steven J. Dick, NASA's Chief Historian) as an essay analyzing the societal impact of space flight. It cites several sources in its endnotes. Its intended audience is those who are interested in the issue beyond the basics, those who want a more in-depth and thoughtful examination of the issue of space flight and its impact.

Therefore, the first would not be appropriate as a secondary source for an academic argument while the second would be good support for such an argument.

Table 2.1: Comparison of Scholarly and Non-Scholarly Sources

Scholarly Sources	Non-Scholarly Sources
Published by credible experts, professional organizations, or governments	Published anonymously, by commercial companies, or by people in the general public
Cites sources	Does not usually cite sources
Uses formal language appropriate for a professional or academic audience	Uses informal language used for general audiences
Usually does not contain advertisements	Often contains advertisements
Usually offers an analysis, argument, or discussion of research	Usually reports facts and lacks an analysis or argument
Usually longer articles of two or more pages	Usually shorter articles of less than three pages

Table 2.1 summarizes some common distinctions between scholarly and non-scholarly sources.

Scholarly articles are often found in "peer-reviewed" journals. These journals target an academic or professional audience (not a general public audience). Academics and professionals submit articles, which are then reviewed by other academics and professionals (their peers). The peers select which articles are published. Published articles are not bought from writers nor do writers "work for" the journals (as is the case for most writers for magazines and newspapers). In summary, articles published in a peer-reviewed journal are not only written by experts, these articles were reviewed by experts who decided that the articles were scholarly and worthwhile to be read by other experts.

Such scholarly sources will "pack a punch" with an academic audience, so use the acronym CAPOW when selecting sources:

- **C**urrency

- **A**uthority

- **P**urpose

- **O**bjectivity

- **W**riting Style

CURRENCY
- Is the source published recently enough to still be relevant to the topic? For example, an article written in 2004 might still be relevant to an argument concerning the Cold War, but an article written in 2004 might not be relevant to an argument concerning the role of social networking in the lives of teenagers because technology and social networks have changed greatly since then.

AUTHORITY
- Is the author a knowledgeable and verifiable expert on the topic?
- Is the source from a reputable publication (peer-reviewed, for instance)?

PURPOSE
- Does the article present an analysis or argument of the topic?
- Does the source insightfully present facts and theories relevant to the topic? For example, if writing about an engineering topic, a paper published in a peer-reviewed

journal published by and read by engineers is going to be more credible than an article about the same topic published in *USA Today*.

OBJECTIVITY

- Does the source fairly present other sides of the issue?

- Does the source not ignore relevant information?

- After cross-checking, does the source use true information as support?

Note, a good source might take a position on an issue and argue in defense of that position. Arguing a position does not mean a source is biased. Bias means unfairly presenting ideas or ignoring information as a way to support an argument.

WRITING STYLE

- Does the source seem to target academics and professionals (not the general public)?

- Is the source written like an essay (not like a bulleted list or summary of ideas)?

- Does the source use and appropriately cite the source it uses?

- Is the language appropriate for an academic audience (for instance, slang is not used)?

- Is the source free from grammar or mechanical errors?

AVOIDING PLAGIARISM

Plagiarism misrepresents a source's words or ideas as your own. To avoid plagiarism, it's best to focus on ways to use research appropriately. Thus, your focus as a writer should be on using research to support ideas, giving credit where credit is due; doing so will make avoiding plagiarism easy.

There are two types of plagiarism. Intentional plagiarism is misrepresenting borrowed material as one's own with the knowledge that doing so is plagiarism, such as copying sentences, paragraphs, or an entire essay from the internet (knowing that doing so is wrong), or hiring another person to write an essay.

Much more common is the second type of plagiarism, which is unintentional. Unintentional plagiarism is failing to cite borrowed material with no intention to misrepresent the material as one's own. Unintentional plagiarism often happens because a paraphrase is too close to the original source's exact words.

Unintentional plagiarism also often happens when a paper includes a works cited page listing each source but fails to include in-text citations to show where each source on the works cited page is used in the essay. "Works cited" literally means "these are the *works cited* in the essay." Every work listed on the works cited page must be cited in the text of the essay and every work cited in the text of the essay must be listed on the works cited page. Failure to do so will cause unintentional plagiarism.

Citations tell the source of the borrowed words or ideas. There are many types of citation formats, such as MLA, APA, Chicago, AP, and many more. Each discipline (science, law, literature, etc.) has its own "style," a little like each country has its own language. The social sciences use APA style, journalism uses APA style, the humanities uses MLA style, and so on.

No matter the citation format, all quotes, paraphrases, and summaries must be cited to avoid plagiarism. All examples here will use MLA style. Consult an MLA style guide for how to cite sources in the text and on the works cited page.

USING RESEARCH
There are three ways to use research:

- Quotes are the borrowed exact words of a source.

- Paraphrases are the borrowed unique information or ideas of a source using all the full and exact details of the original, but not the exact words.

- Summaries are the borrowed unique information or ideas of a source in shortened or abbreviated form.

QUOTATIONS

Use quotations (1) to emphasize specific word choices and (2) to avoid potentially misrepresenting the idea of the original source.

To avoid plagiarism, quotations must:

- be put in quotation marks

- be cited in the sentence text

- have the full source cited on the works cited page

For example:

Acceptable Quotation:

Manfred Kroger said, "Unintentional plagiarism is often the excuse by an offender."

Plagiarism:

Example 1: Manfred Kroger said unintentional plagiarism is often the excuse by an offender.

Example 2: Unintentional plagiarism is often the excuse by an offender.

Although the first example of plagiarism mentions the author's name in the sentence as the in-text citation, the words are not in quotation marks, so it is still plagiarism. The implication is that this sentence is a paraphrase of what Kroger said instead of his exact words, which is unintentional plagiarism. The second example of plagiarism might be intentional or unintentional, but failure to put the exact words in quotation marks and cite the source in the sentence results in plagiarism.

Remember, although avoiding plagiarism when quoting is important, using quotations effectively to support ideas is the goal. In fact, quotations should rarely be more than a few words since the purpose of quoting is to emphasize only exact words. For example:

Weak Use of Quotation:

> According to the U.S. Department of Education, "The evaluators found that some schools were excited and committed to using the Web site's resources, but were underutilizing it because they lacked sufficient structures, such as training and time for teachers to learn about its offerings, internal communication mechanisms to track student progress, and adequate technical support."

Strong Use of Quotation:

> According to the U.S. Department of Education, despite being "excited and committed" about the website, some schools were "underutilizing" it due to a lack of proper training, funding, and other structures.

Although both quotations are properly cited (so neither is plagiarized), by using just a few words in quotations, those exact words are more emphasized to the reader in the strong example, and emphasis on exact words is the purpose of quoting.

Also, avoid "dumped" or "hanging" quotations, which are sentences that are only quotations. For example:

"Dumped" or "Hanging" Quotation:

> "The evaluators found that some schools were excited and committed to using the Web site's resources, but were underutilizing it because they lacked sufficient

structures, such as training and time for teachers to learn about its offerings, internal communication mechanisms to track student progress, and adequate technical support" (U.S. Department of Education).

Strong Use of Quotation:

Despite being "excited and committed" about the website, some schools were "underutilizing" it due to a lack of proper training, funding, and other structures. (U.S. Department of Education).

Again, the "dumped" or "hanging" quotation example is not plagiarized, but the strong use of quotation puts the emphasis on key words from the original quotation, and the purpose of quotation is to provide such emphasis on specific word choices.

PARAPHRASES

Paraphrases are used when the exact words of the original source do not need to be emphasized. The purpose of paraphrasing is (1) to maintain the voice of the writer, (2) to demonstrate how the ideas (not the exact words) are relevant, and (3) to demonstrate the writer's comprehension by being able accurately to restate the original source's meaning. Statistics and unique opinions are most often paraphrased. To avoid plagiarism, all paraphrases must:

- be cited in the sentence
- have the full source cited on the works cited page

The idea shown by statistics (and not the exact words of the statistics) is important, so statistics should almost always be paraphrased instead of directly quoted. For example:

Original Words from Source:

"A review of empirical studies of plagiarism from as early as 1941 through until 2005 shows varied statistics regarding the extent and intensity of plagiarism – from as few as 20% of students to as high as 75% of students engaging in plagiarism of some

form."

Plagiarism:

- As many as 75% of students or as low as 20% of students plagiarize.

- Empirical studies of plagiarism from 1941 to 2005 found that as few as 20% and as

  many as 75% of students engage in plagiarism (Jones).

In the first example of plagiarism, the reader can not tell where the information in the

sentence comes from. Even if the source is listed on the works cited page, without a citation

in the sentence, this is plagiarism. In the second example of plagiarism, a citation is

provided, but the word choice is too close to the original words from the source. This is an

acceptable paraphrase:

Acceptable Paraphrase:

The number of students who plagiarize in some form varies from 20% to 75%

according to several studies from 1941 through 2005 (Jones).

When a unique opinion has no words that need to be emphasized, then a paraphrase should

be used. For example:

Original Words from Source:

"Teachers' requirements to cite a minimum number and certain types of sources

encouraged third party fraud."

Plagiarism:

1. The requirements of teachers to use a minimum amount and certain kinds of sources

   encouraged third party fraud (Balingit 18).

2. Teachers' requirements to use a minimum number of citations and certain types of

   sources encouraged plagiarism (Balingit 18).

Although both of the examples of plagiarism are cited, both use word choices that are too close to the original words from the source. This is an acceptable paraphrase:

Acceptable Paraphrase:

> Students sometimes feel the need to plagiarize because they are required to use a specified number of sources of a certain type (Balingit 18).

Fear of writing a paraphrase that is too close to the original words from the source often leads to wanting to use quotations only instead of paraphrases. However, remember that quotations and paraphrases serve different purposes. Paraphrases should be used to demonstrate to the audience a full and complete understanding of the ideas relevant to the issue, which means being able to express those ideas in your own words. A sign of good comprehension is not repeating exactly verbatim a quotation but of using one's own words to express the same idea. Also, readers tend to skim long quotations since the reader's intent is to understand the writer's ideas. Readers tend to read paraphrases more closely as they use the writer's own words. (If the reader wanted to read the long, original words from the source, the reader could go read that original source.)

To avoid plagiarism when writing a paraphrase, read the original two or three times to understand its meaning. Then, don't look at the original. Wait a few minutes (or longer). Then, without looking at the original, write your expression of the idea of the original. Finally, check your paraphrase against the original to ensure that the paraphrase has not just changed a few words and no more than three words in a row (excluding articles or prepositions) are used. (If three or more words in a row are used, then put quotation marks around them.)

When writing a paraphrase, also be sure the paraphrase accurately captures the idea of the original source, being careful not to add your opinion. For example:

Original Words from Source:

"Indeed, according to humanists, self-evaluation is the only meaningful test of whether learning has taken place."

Incorrect Paraphrases:

1. Humanists correctly believe that only self-evaluation will assess learning success (Kanuka 107).

2. Humanists believe that self-evaluation will assess learning success (Kanuka 107).

The use of the single word "correctly" in the first incorrect paraphrase has added an opinion to this otherwise acceptable paraphrase. The paraphrase mistakenly asserts that Kanuka included the opinion that the humanists are "correct" in their beliefs, so the paraphrase is inaccurate. The second incorrect paraphrase leaves out part of the meaning of the original source, namely that self-evaluation is the "only" way to assess learning in a meaningful way. By omitting that single idea, the paraphrase is misrepresenting Kanuka's assertion. This is an acceptable paraphrase:

Acceptable Paraphrase:

Humanists believe that only self-evaluation will appropriately assess learning success (Kanuka 107).

Another common error that leads to unintentional plagiarism is to "save up" a citation till the end of a paragraph or till the end of several sentences. However, to avoid plagiarism, cite EVERY sentence that is a paraphrase. For example:

Original Words from Source:

"While there will always be a need for authoritative oversight, the responsibility for research integrity ultimately lies in the hands of the scientific community. Educators and advisors must ensure that the students they mentor understand the importance of scientific integrity."

Plagiarism:

Despite the importance of oversight, the scientific community has the final responsibility for ensuring its own research integrity. Instructors and administrators must make certain that their students recognize the importance of academic and professional integrity in science (Long et al. 1294).

Although the second sentence is correctly cited, the first sentence has no citation, so it is likely unintentional plagiarism. The implication is that the first sentence is the writer's original idea but it is really an idea that comes from Long et al. This is an acceptable paraphrase:

Acceptable Paraphrase:

Despite the importance of oversight, Long et al. insist the scientific community has the final responsibility for ensuring its own research integrity (1294). Instructors and administrators must make certain that their students recognize the importance of academic and professional integrity in science (Long et al. 1294).

Finally, the paraphrase should be about the same length as the original. Do not condense or leave out details when writing a paraphrase.

SUMMARIES

Summaries are like paraphrases because they tell the same idea of the original source in your own words. However, the distinction between summaries and paraphrases is that summaries provide a condensed version of those ideas, leaving out unnecessary details. Summaries might condense an entire article or section of an article into one paragraph or a few sentences. To avoid plagiarism, all summaries must:

- be cited in the sentence

- have the full source cited on the works cited page

Introduction sections, conclusion sections, and abstracts are often good places to start for key ideas that may warrant a summary in an essay. For example:

Original Words from Source:

> Another issue regarding the prevention of cheating is that the fact that cheating hinders education does not mean that putting an end to it will automatically improve education. Those students who want to get passable grades with as little work as possible are unlikely to start studying hard just because they can no longer cheat. What hinders education is not cheating but the underlying lack of motivation: fighting cheating may only address a superficial symptom. And if curbing cheating does not have a major positive impact on learning then the fact that cheating hinders learning cannot justify fighting it.

Plagiarism:

> Cheating is only a symptom of a student's lack of motivation to learn. Education will not improve by preventing cheating, so punishing cheating only because it hurts learning is not warranted (Bouville 74-5).

Although the second sentence is cited, the first sentence is not, resulting in plagiarism, which is probably unintentional. The implication is that the first sentence is the writer's original idea and the second sentence is a paraphrase from Bouville. Here is an acceptable summary:

Acceptable Summary:

> According to Mathieu Bouville, cheating is only a symptom of a student's lack of motivation to learn (74-5). He asserts, therefore, that education will not improve by

preventing cheating, so punishing cheating only because it hurts learning is not

warranted (74-5).

Note that each sentence of the summary indicates the source of that sentence. (Using "he"

as a pronoun in the second sentence is an acceptable citation because the pronoun refers

to Mathieu Bouville from the first sentence.)

Scientific studies or results as well as lengthy presentation of statistics are commonly

summarized. For example:

Original Chart:

National Center for Education Statistics

Acceptable Summary:

Between 2002 and 2005, high school distance education enrollments increased by

about 30% while elementary distance education enrollments increased by 400%

(National Center for Education Statistics).

COMMON KNOWLEDGE

Facts or widely-accepted ideas that are not likely to be doubted or debated to be true

are common knowledge. Examples of common knowledge might be dates of historical

events, biographical information, and observable facts.

For example, both of the following statements are common knowledge that would not

need to be cited:

- George Washington was the first president of the United States.

- Some people claim that George Washington was not the first president of the United

States.

Both are statements of fact. Although you may not have known the second fact, it does not need to be cited because it is a statement of fact that is agreed upon by several sources. Therefore, this statement is common knowledge and does not need to be cited.

In contrast, consider this example:

Although John Hanson was first in power under the Articles of Confederation, this union of the States was "more like NATO than the USA" according to Richard Norton Smith, a biographer of Washington (qtd. in Schulte). Therefore, Hanson was not the first president; Washington was.

This example does need to be cited because it uses the original idea of Richard Norton Smith about the Articles of Confederation. According to Smith, this union of states was "more like NATO than the USA." This is a unique opinion, not to mention a direct quotation, so it must be cited. (Note that the example here uses an indirect citation, which means that in the source written by Schulte, Schulte quotes from Richard Norton Smith. This sentence uses the quotation from Richard Norton Smith, so "qtd. in," which stands for "quoted in," is used in the citation. The citation says that Smith is quoted in Schulte and that the source written by Schulte is on the works cited page.) In this same example, note that the final sentence is not the opinion of Smith or of Schulte. It does not need to be cited because it is the writer's conclusion reached from the research presented.

Common knowledge will likely be encountered during preliminary research. Common sources of common knowledge are encyclopedias and dictionaries. The information in these sources is agreed upon by the experts.

Do not cite common knowledge unless you believe that the audience might doubt the idea as being true. The citation provides a way for the audience to find out more to assure themselves that the fact presented is actually true. For example, consider this sentence:

United States copyright law protects expression of form and not ideas or facts. This sentence is a fact, common knowledge, so it does not need to be cited. However, if the audience might doubt this interpretation of the copyright law and what it does and does not protect, then it should be cited:

United States copyright law protects expression of form and not ideas or facts (17 USC 102).

Common knowledge should be put into your own words (like a paraphrase or summary), but because it is common knowledge, it does not need to be cited.

Of course, is any idea truly "original" or "unique?" For example, consider this quotation: "Plagiarism is a form of cheating and academic misconduct." This is a quote of a fact. Both of the following plagiarize:

- Plagiarism is a form of cheating and academic misconduct.
- Plagiarism is a type of cheating and academic misconduct.

Both examples of plagiarism are too close to the exact words of the original quotation.

Put the idea into your own words, and no citation is then needed because it is a fact. Here is an acceptable presentation of this common knowledge fact:

Plagiarism is cheating and a violation of academic integrity.

Although this sentence is "like" a paraphrase of the original words from the source, this is not a unique idea owned by the source. The words are substantially changed, so they are now a unique creation. The idea is common knowledge (a fact) and the words are original, so it is not plagiarism even though it is not cited.

However, in all cases, **if in doubt, CITE.**

Integrating Research

Citing research is necessary to give credit where credit is due, but also smoothly integrate research to demonstrate how the research supports your ideas.

Tell how the research relates to your ideas. Do not assume the quotation, paraphrase, or summary is self-explanatory. How does the research prove your point? How should the reader interpret the research in relation to your ideas? For example, each of the following examples integrates the same quotation to serve very different purposes:

- The problem is so severe that President Obama described it as "debilitating."

- Even though President Obama described the problem as "debilitating," the problem is really not so severe because....

- President Obama described it as "debilitating," which shows the national level of public awareness about this problem.

Also, the first time a source is used, tell the source's authority. In the previous example, President Obama is well-known, so who he is does not need to be explained. Similarly, as president, his opinion about a problem affecting the country would be relevant. However, the credibility and relevancy of a source's opinion to the issue at hand is often not so clear, so it must be established.

Establish credibility of a source by telling the author's background experience relevant to the topic. For example:

John Smith, Harvard economist, argues the recession is "temporary at best." Another way to establish credibility is by telling what the author wrote or where the author published the work. For example:

- John Smith, author of "The New Economy," argues the recession is "temporary at best."

- John Smith in *The Economist* argues the recession is "temporary at best."

It's assumed that someone who published a scholarly article must have some amount of authority on the topic. The person must have researched the topic in order to publish a scholarly article about it. Thus, telling the title of the article or the title of the scholarly journal where the article was published establishes the author's credibility on the topic.

There is no need to establish credibility if the author is unknown and the title shows authority. For example:

The recession is "temporary at best" ("The New Economy").

Also, there is no need to establish credibility if the author is an organization whose very name shows authority on the subject. For example:

The United Nations Economic Commission for Europe argues the recession is "temporary at best."

CONCLUSION

To wrap up, begin research with an open mind to discover more about a topic. Use research questions and test a variety of keywords to focus research. Do not limit yourself to internet search engines, and instead focus on free scholarly journals and, most importantly, the abundance of academic resources available through the school's library. However the research is found, evaluate sources carefully to assure that each is scholarly in nature and will be persuasive for an academic audience.

Integrate research to demonstrate the credibility of sources and how each source supports the overall ideas of the paper. To avoid plagiarism and effectively use research to support ideas in an academic paper, remember these key strategies:

- Include in-text citations to define clearly for your reader which sentences are quotations, paraphrases, or summaries and which sentences are your own ideas.

- Include a works cited page that lists full publication information for all works cited in the sentences of the paper.

- If three or more nouns, verbs, adjectives, or adverbs are in a row, then it is a quotation and requires quotation marks.

- Quote only when the author or exact words are important to emphasize.

- Do not look at the original words when paraphrasing. Express the idea in your own words.

- Do not cite common knowledge, but if in doubt about whether something is common knowledge or not, cite. It's better to have an unnecessary citation than to plagiarize unintentionally!

QUESTIONS TO CONSIDER

1. What sources would provide good preliminary research?

2. How does preliminary research help in developing research questions and keywords?

3. How can search engines, online academic journals and web portals, and the library be used to find secondary sources?

4. What is a scholarly source?

5. How do citations avoid plagiarism?

6. When should a quotation be used instead of a paraphrase?

7. What distinguishes a paraphrase that must be cited from common knowledge that does not?

8. How can quotations, paraphrases, and summaries be integrated to best support ideas in an academic paper?

Works Cited

Balingit, JoAnn. "Internet Plagiarism as Flashpoint and Folklore." University of Oregon, 2009.

Web. 1 Apr. 2012.

Bouville, Mathieu. "Why Is Cheating Wrong?" *Studies in Philosophy & Education* 29.1

(2010): 67-76. *Education Research Complete*. Web. 1 Apr. 2012.

Dick, Stephen J. "The Societal Impact of Space Flight." *ASK Magazine*, Fall 2008. Web. 1

Apr. 2012.

Jones, Michael. "Back-translation: The Latest Form of Plagiarism." University of Wollongong,

2009. Web. 1 Apr. 2012.

Kanuka, Heather. "Understanding E-Learning Technologies-in-Practice through Philosophies-

in-Practice." *The Theory and Practice of Online Learning*. 2nd ed. Ed. Terry Anderson.

Edmonton, AB: AU Press, 2008. 91-120. Print.

Kroger, Manfred. "Editorial: Some Thoughts on Plagiarism." *Comprehensive Reviews in Food

Science and Safety* 9.3 (May 2010): 259-60. Web. 1 Apr. 2012.

Long, Tara C. et al. "Responding to Possible Plagiarism." *Science* 322 (2009): 1293-1294.

Print.

National Aeronautics and Space Administration (NASA). "International Space Station: Facts

and Figures." *NASA*. NASA, n.d. Web. 1 Apr. 2012.

National Center for Education Statistics. *2009 Digest of Education Statistics*. NCES, May

2009. Web. 1 Apr. 2012.

Schulte, Bret. "Washington? Get in Line." *USA Today,* 6 Aug. 2006. Web. 1 Apr. 2012.

17 USC Sec. 102. 2011. Print.

U.S. Department of Education. "Evaluating Online Learning: Challenges and Strategies for

Success." *U.S. Department of Education*, July 2008. Web. 1 Apr. 2012.

CHAPTER 3: CONSTRUCTING CREDIBLE ARGUMENTS, READING CRITICALLY, AND WRITING EFFECTIVELY

INTRODUCTION

Lesson three emphasizes creating and supporting credible arguments. Convincing arguments most often utilize persuasive appeals, which will be discussed at length in this lesson. Argumentative fallacies will also be discussed, which will help you avoid committing these fallacies in your writing. By learning these persuasive appeals and fallacies, you will not only understand how to incorporate these appeals into a strong argument and how to avoid fallacies in your writing, but you will also strengthen your critical reading skills in order to help you find strong, academic research. Finally, this lesson will show you how to properly revise your work, create strong thesis statements, and introduce and conclude an essay in a thoughtful manner.

PERSUASIVE APPEALS

You are interviewing two contractors to do a renovation on your house. One arrives well-groomed and on time with a binder of references, photographs of previously completed jobs, and evidence of current licenses and certifications. The other contractor arrives looking slightly disheveled and ten minutes late, and he tells you that references can be provided, handwrites a list of addresses of previous jobs, and verbally confirms current licenses and certifications. Which contractor are you more likely to hire?

Although both may have just as good references, experience, and credentials, you are more likely to hire the first contractor who arrived on time and looking professional with full evidence of past work and qualifications. Similarly, readers are more likely to believe an argument when it is logically presented in a way that makes the audience trust the author as a respectful and knowledgeable person. Even if two arguments are exactly the same in terms of the reasons and conclusion presented, the argument that carries the most appeal will be most convincing.

What makes an argument appealing then? Aristotle long ago identified three appeals:

- Pathos

- Ethos

- Logos

PATHOS

An **appeal to pathos (emotions)** relies on the audience's emotions and feelings. As children, the first type of persuasive appeal we encounter is an appeal to pathos, such as "If you don't go to the ceremony, you will break your mother's heart" or "Behave or you will receive a spanking." The first is an appeal to love and the second an appeal to fear.

Such appeals to emotions seem manipulative, and they are when used alone instead of to supplement an argument that also carries logical appeal. For instance, in an argument supporting a ban on smoking in public places, a writer might present statistics that demonstrate the serious negative health effects of second-hand smoke. Those effects will appeal to people's emotions—their fear—but those effects also provide logical reasons to support the argument.

Stephen E. Lucas, in <u>"The Stylistic Artistry of the Declaration of Independence,"</u> for instance, evaluates Thomas Jefferson's use of such emotional appeals by noting the emotional content of Jefferson's word choices:

> Whereas the first twenty-two grievances describe the king's acts with such temperate verbs as "refused," "called together," "dissolved," "endeavored," "made," "erected," "kept," and "affected," the war grievances use emotionally charged verbs such as "plundered," "ravaged," "burnt," and "destroyed."

Such word choices were used to create more support for the revolution by targeting people in America who had not yet experienced the economic and political difficulties by emotionally depicting these struggles and thus creating an appeal to people's anger and resentment (Lucas).

ETHOS

An **appeal to ethos (ethics)** relies on the credibility of the author. Essentially, audiences trust writers who appear to be ethical, trustworthy, and know what they are talking about.

A writer demonstrates ethics by being fair and objective, even while presenting an argument on an issue. While a biased writer might misrepresent or ignore relevant opinions or facts about an issue that oppose the writer's argument, an ethical writer will fairly present such opinions and facts even if the writer disagrees with these opinions or about what the facts mean. By presenting and discussing such opposing facts or opinions, the ethical writer demonstrates that the issue has been fairly, objectively, and fully considered, making audiences more likely to trust the conclusions reached.

For example, a writer arguing against the use of the death penalty might mention the reasons proponents have for supporting the death penalty, such as the need for retribution and deterrence. By mentioning such opposing arguments, the writer demonstrates awareness of the complexities of the issue and shows due respect to others who have good reasons for supporting the death penalty. The writer can then go on to discuss the flaws or limitations of such arguments or offer compromises or concessions in support of the argument against the death penalty. As a result, the writer's argument against the death penalty is more persuasive, even for those who support the death penalty, because the writer has demonstrated fairness and extensive knowledge about the issue.

Demonstrating knowledge about an issue builds the writer's credibility and overall appeal to ethos. In a nutshell, audiences trust writers who demonstrate experience in what they are writing about. A writer can demonstrate knowledge by revealing personal background, educational accomplishments, or professional experience. For example, investors reading a proposed business plan for a new restaurant will be more likely to be persuaded to invest in that restaurant if that business plan includes details of the owners' past history working in other restaurants.

Writers might not have personal experience with a topic, which is often the case in student essays. In such situations, writers build credibility by using good sources that themselves have credibility in the topic! (See the discussion of evaluating sources in Lesson 2.)

When using research, establish the credibility of the sources the first time a source is used by mentioning the author's experiences or background in the topic, such as by mentioning the author's education, professional experience, or publication(s) relating to the subject matter. For example:

Weak:

John Smith argues the recession is "temporary at best."

Strong:

1. John Smith, Harvard economist, argues the recession is "temporary at best."

2. John Smith, author of "The New Economy," argues the recession is "temporary at best."

3. John Smith in *The Economist* argues the recession is "temporary at best."

The weak example carries no appeal because the reader has no idea who John Smith is. It could be the writer's neighbor for all the reader knows! However, in each of the strong examples, John Smith's opinion about the recession carries more credibility because the first mentions his experience as an economist, the second mentions the title of his publication on the economy, and the third mentions the title of the professional economics publication where he published. (Titles of publications can establish credibility because it's assumed that if someone has published on a topic, then that person has researched and become knowledgeable about that topic. This assumption only holds true, however, if the sources have been evaluated successfully by the writer!)

In the strong examples, the experience and authority of the author encourages the audience to trust him as a reliable source with a trustworthy opinion about economic subject matter. The writer who uses this source likewise establishes credibility on the subject even though the writer may not have any professional or educational experience in economics. By using credible sources and demonstrating their credibility, the writer builds credibility with the audience as someone who has researched the topic thoroughly and become well-informed and knowledgeable, even though the writer may not have direct personal or professional experience in the subject matter.

A writer can further demonstrate trustworthiness through word choice. People trust others who seem to be similar. Avoid "you" because it distances the audience from the writer, making the audience feel separate from rather than connected with the writer. For example:

Weak:

> You should not underestimate this problem.

Strong:

> This problem should not be underestimated.

> We should not underestimate this problem.

The weak example seems more of an order and implies that it is only the reader that needs to not underestimate the problem. The strong examples are more objective about what we all should do.

Thus, using "we" and "us" instead of "you" or "I" can build a sense of community or bond between the writer and audience. For example:

Weak:

> The first thing you need to do is find out which websites your children are using.

Strong:

> The first thing we need to do is find out which websites our children are using.

The weak example sounds a bit accusatory toward "you" in the audience while the strong example sounds more inclusive as if the solution requires a communal effort. Audiences respond to such inclusiveness.

Using the Declaration of Independence as an example again, Lucas notes Jefferson's distinction between the British "them" and the collective "we" of the colonists, acting as one force and entity, in such statements as "*we* mutually pledge to each other *our* Lives, *our* Fortunes and *our* sacred Honor." The result, as Lucas summarizes, is that Jefferson:

reduces the psychic distance between the reader and the text and coaxes the reader into seeing the dispute with Great Britain through the eyes of the revolutionaries. As the drama of the Declaration unfolds, the reader is increasingly solicited to identify with Congress and "the good People of these Colonies," to share their sense of victimage, to participate vicariously in their struggle, and ultimately to act with them in their heroic quest for freedom.

Thus, Jefferson establishes credibility for the people authoring this declaration as seeking the best interest of all colonists, persuading the audience to seek independence together.

Logos

An **appeal to logos (logic)** relies on the sound logic of the argument. Although we often think of an "argument" as a debate or a heated discussion, in terms of logic, an argument is simply statements of reasons (premises) in support of a conclusion. An argument is considered "logical" if the reasons "add up" to the conclusion being true or probably true. For example:

Reason: I am a human.

Reason: Humans are mortal.

Conclusion: I am mortal.

In this argument, the reasons are true and the reasons being true necessitate that the conclusion must be true too. Therefore, the argument is logical.

An argument is considered logical when the reasons are true AND the reasons being true necessitate the conclusion to be true or make the conclusion probably true. Again, two conditions must be met for a logical appeal to be successful:

1. reasons are proven to be true, AND

2. the reasons being true make the conclusion true, or probably true, too.

Why use "probably true?" Very few arguments can be proven with absolute certainty. For instance, if we hear a doorbell ring, we instinctually believe someone is at the door because internally we've built the following argument:

Reason: I've heard the doorbell.

Reason: A doorbell ringing means someone is at the door.

Conclusion: Someone is at the door.

If we get to the door and no one is there, we are temporarily surprised because the logical argument supporting our conclusion that someone is at the door has been proven wrong. The conclusion that "someone is at the door" that we believed to be certainly true from our internal argument was not actually true.

However, although this conclusion was proven to be wrong, the argument was still logical! The argument really only proved that it is "probably" true that someone is at the door based on past experiences of people being at the door when doorbells have rung.

Most scientific arguments are based on what is probably true based on past observations and experiences. For example, the belief that smoking causes cancer is based on observations of cancer rates among smokers compared to cancer rates among non-smokers. Although not all smokers will develop cancer, the conclusion that smoking causes cancer is probably true based on the observations.

The reason some debates, like abortion or capital punishment, seem to be endless is because both sides have logically appealing arguments. For example, one logical argument against legalized abortion might be:

Reason: Abortion kills a fetus.

Reason: A fetus is human.

Reason: Killing of humans is murder.

Conclusion: Therefore, abortion is murder.

One logical argument supporting legalized abortion might be:

Reason: Abortion kills a fetus

Reason: A fetus is not human.

Reason: Only killing of humans is murder.

Conclusion: Therefore, abortion is not murder.

Both are valid arguments because if the reasons are true, then the conclusion must be necessarily true too. The burden in each argument is in proving whether or not the fetus is actually a human. Because proving this point is difficult to do with any certainty is just one reason why the abortion debate continues.

A logical appeal is successfully made if the argument is valid and does the best possible job of proving that each reason is, in fact, true. As demonstrated in the abortion arguments with the debate about whether a fetus is or is not a human, some reasons used in arguments can not be proven to be certainly true, at least not for all audiences, which is why Rogerian and middle ground persuasive strategies have emerged. These strategies of argumentation purposefully seek to find an accommodation, compromise, or consensus while accepting that some aspects of the debate cannot be resolved. (See the discussion of Rogerian and middle ground argumentation strategies in Lessons 6 through 8.)

To continue with the Declaration of Independence as an example, its argument logically supports the need for revolution by putting forth several reasons enumerated by Lucas:

Proposition 1: All men are created equal.

Proposition 2: They [all men, from proposition 1] are endowed by their creator with certain unalienable rights.

Proposition 3: Among these [man's unalienable rights, from proposition 2] are life, liberty, and the pursuit of happiness.

Proposition 4: To secure these rights [man's unalienable rights, from propositions 2 and 3] governments are instituted among men.

Proposition 5: Whenever any form of government becomes destructive of these ends [securing man's unalienable rights, from propositions 2-4], it is the right of the people to alter or to abolish it.

Each of these propositions is a general assumption or warrant (a debatable idea and not an observable fact). (See the discussion of warrants and assumptions used in Toulmin argumentation in Lesson 4.) Jefferson then goes on to provide evidence to demonstrate how the English government has violated these listed rights. If each proposition and the evidence about the English government's violations are proven true to the audience, then the audience has no other choice than to accept the logical conclusion of the argument, which is that the American people must "alter" or "abolish" the English government of the colonies.

EVALUATING APPEALS AND IDENTIFYING FALLACIOUS REASONING

When evaluating an argument, the goal is to determine if the argument makes the conclusion probably true. To do that, determine if the reasons have been proven to be true and if them being true makes the conclusion probably true as well. An argument is called "valid" if the reasons being true make the conclusion true. An argument is called "logical" if it is a valid argument AND the reasons are, in fact, actually true.

Illogical arguments that use all truthful reasons and conclusions are sometimes difficult to spot! The truthfulness of the conclusion makes us want to believe the validity of the argument. For example, consider this argument:

In a recent study, a group of 100 people were provided with weight training and nutritional guidance. After two months, significant weight loss was observed among the majority of the people, leading researchers to conclude that weight training and good nutrition are an important aspect of weight management.

Because the conclusion is likely true ("weight training and good nutrition are an important aspect of weight management") and we have no reason to doubt the reasons (the actual results of the study), we may want to claim the argument has a strong logical appeal. However, do the reasons of this argument (not our own observations or other research about weight management) prove the conclusion to be true? How do we know that it wasn't weight training alone or nutritional guidance alone that caused the weight loss in this group of people? The conclusion insists that it was the two combined, but the same results might have been observed if either one or the other had been used, so the argument has a weak logical appeal even though all the statements made might be true.

When evaluating arguments, look for such fallacies of reasoning. Sometimes these flaws are accidental; sometimes they are committed on purpose. It's useful, then, to be familiar with a few common types of logical fallacies.

Non Sequitur

Non sequitur, literally meaning "it does not follow" in Latin, is a logical fallacy where the conclusion is not the logical next step from the reasons. For example:

Surgeon General warnings should be removed from cigarettes because many people have lived to be in their 90s who have smoked for most of their lives.

Remember, arguments often only prove that the conclusion is "probably" and not "certainly" true. The number of cases of lung cancer associated with smoking proves a causal connection between the two. It does not follow that because some people die of other causes first that there is no connection between cancer and smoking.

HASTY GENERALIZATION

A hasty generalization reaches a conclusion based on too little evidence. Any type of stereotyping of a group of anything is using a hasty generalization. For example:

> I owned a Sony computer and it broke within the first week, so Sony products are
> simply not very well made.

Just one example is not sufficient to prove the conclusion that all are the same way. Personal experience might provide a very good demonstration of an ethical appeal to show direct knowledge, but supplementing that personal experience with more evidence from a broader sample is necessary for the conclusion to be logically supported.

SWEEPING GENERALIZATION

A sweeping generalization oversimplifies a correlation. Essentially, such a fallacy ignores common exceptions. For example:

> Students are assessed by the quality of their work, so this assessment process
> should be a part of their learning. If students are allowed to retake tests, then their
> course grades will improve because they will learn from each assessment.

Although the conclusion might be true, the argument makes a sweeping generalization about how students learn. Tests might be just a small fraction of the overall course grade or students might better learn from non-testing assessments. The proposed solution is a sweeping generalization of the nature of tests and the way students learn.

A blanket statement is a type of severe sweeping generalization. A blanket statement asserts that all or none of a specific group is a certain way. For example, "the only way to increase employee productivity is to restrict access to some websites" or "students should never be allowed to drop out of high school." If the reader can think of just one other way to increase employee productivity (such as allowing employees frequent breaks) or one single situation where a specific student should be allowed to drop out of high school (such as to get a GED and support a family), then the argument has been proven wrong.

Some key words to avoid blanket statements are "never," "none," "no one," "always," "all," "everyone," and the like. Similarly, some nouns alone might indicate a blanket statement, such as "French women are promiscuous," Avoid such words by being precise, using words like "frequently," "occasionally," "sometimes," "many," "some," and other words that leave room for exceptions.

FALSE ANALOGY

A false analogy argues that since two things are similar in one way, then they must be similar in another way or all ways. For example:

> She did a great job of balancing the budget at that company, so we should elect her as mayor.

Although companies and governments both have budgets, they have significant differences in purposes. Is balancing the budget the primary goal of a city mayor? The similarity between the company and government budget does not logically support that she will have the ability to be successful in the overall job of mayor.

FALSE AUTHORITY

A false authority is exactly as it sounds: using a source that is not a true authority on the matter. This is actually a common unintentional fallacy when a general information web source is used to support a claim rather than using a true authority on the matter.

For example, using Wikipedia to support a claim uses the false authority logical fallacy. It's illogical to trust Wikipedia information any more than to trust a neighbor's assertion on the same topic since anyone with an Internet connection can modify a Wikipedia article. Again, the information might be accurate, but being true is not the same thing as being logical.

AD HOMINEM (ATTACK THE PERSON)

Ad hominem, literally meaning "to the man" in Latin, is a fallacy that attacks a person rather than the ideas or argument of that person. We see a lot of this type of fallacious logic in the "mud slinging" campaigns of certain politicians. For example:

> That man couldn't even keep his teenage daughter from getting pregnant, so you know he won't be a good police commissioner.

Is the politician's family life in this case truly relevant to whether or not he'd be a good police commissioner? The person is being attacked rather than reasons provided for why he would not be a good police commissioner.

BANDWAGON

A bandwagon logical fallacy asserts that something should be believed because most people already believe it. For example:

> It should be legal to download movies because everyone is doing it and the companies know it's being done on a regular basis.

There may be many good arguments to support the free sharing of entertainment online, but the argument presented that it should be legal because everyone is doing it is illogical.

CIRCULAR REASONING (BEGGING THE QUESTION)

Begging the question uses the premises of the argument as the conclusion. It uses circular reasoning to claim that something is true rather than demonstrating why or how it is true. Often the conclusion is simply a restatement of one or more of the reasons. For example:

He could not be guilty of that crime because it's just not in his nature.

Why is it not in his nature? What about his nature makes it probably true that he could not be guilty? The reason leads to more questions that "beg" for the conclusion to be supported with actual reasons.

FALSE DILEMMA

False dilemma, also known as the either/or fallacy, poses a choice between two things without acknowledging any other alternatives. For example:

How could anyone who cares about our country and its people oppose health care reform?

Essentially only two options are presented here: (1) care about the country and its people or (2) oppose health care reform. The rhetorical question implies that people who care about the country and its people must support health care reform, omitting the option that some people might care about the country and its people and still oppose health care reform. Rhetorical questions should be carefully assessed and used to determine if the answer the reader is asked to provide is not part of a logical fallacy.

POST HOC ERGO PROPTER HOC

Post hoc ergo propter hoc, literally meaning "after this therefore because of this" in Latin, assumes that there is a cause and effect relationship between two events because one occurred before the other. For example:

> The moment prayer was removed from schools, society has seen an increase in teenage pregnancy and violence on school campuses. School prayer should be reinstituted because it can help protect our children.

Concluding that prayer is a solution to these teen problems is not logically supported by the argument. Many other changes in society and schools occurred in the same time period since school prayer was removed, so one or a combination of these changes may have contributed to these problems. Just because one event occurred before the other does not mean that the earlier event must have caused the later one. There needs to be more support for the conclusion to show the causal relationship.

SLIPPERY SLOPE

A slippery slope argues that one thing will automatically lead to another. There is usually some sort of causal connection between the two things, but this connection is usually just possible and not very probable. For example:

> Legalizing marijuana will lead to more crime and drug addiction.

This argument is fallacious if no additional support is provided. Although more crime and drug addiction may be possible, this argument has not demonstrated that it is probable.

RED HERRING

The red herring fallacy introduces an unrelated topic that is usually controversial. For example:

Hitler forcibly aborted children to perform medical experiments, and we would be no better than he if we allowed aborted fetuses to be used for medical research. Bringing up Hitler is not relevant to the argument that seeks to determine whether or not research should be performed on aborted fetuses. Bringing up Hitler sidetracks the argument from the actual issue.

USING PERSUASIVE APPEALS IN ACADEMIC ESSAYS

The purpose of an argument is not to tell an audience what you believe, but to persuade the audience that your belief is a good one. When making an argument, the goal should be to persuade the audience using the rhetorical appeals of pathos, ethos, and logos.

We've seen through the analysis of the Declaration of Independence how the rhetorical appeals can work together within the same argument. Jefferson built credibility through word choices that united the colonists while appealing to their emotions to supplement the logical argument that supported independence.

Proving reasons to be true should be based on good use of research or personal observations and experiences. For example, if arguing that capital punishment should not be legal because it does not actually deter crime, it would be necessary to present credible research to prove crime is not significantly deterred by the death penalty. Some credible research asserts the opposite, that the death penalty does deter crime. Therefore, for the argument to be logically appealing, it would be necessary to discuss this competing research and prove that the research supporting the claim that the death penalty does not deter crime is more persuasive. Using research and addressing the opposition in a fair and objective way is making an ethical appeal (building credibility) while also serving to create the logical appeal of the argument.

Another way to build both an appeal to logos and ethos is to avoid logical fallacies. Obviously, doing so builds a logical appeal, but avoiding logical fallacies also builds credibility by demonstrating to the audience that the issue has been fairly considered and the writer has not taken any shortcuts by using logical fallacies.

In an academic argument, emotional appeals are typically most effective as "hooks" in the introduction paragraph to grab the reader's attention, making the reader see the importance of the issue. For instance, a few sentences telling a vivid short story describing a pet's final moments before being euthanized in an animal shelter might make for an effective emotional appeal to begin an argument essay in support of no-kill shelters. However, emotional appeals through vivid language and examples can be used throughout an essay to supplement the logical appeal of the overall argument.

Emotional appeals are typically best to motivate for an action rather than to persuade an audience to believe an idea. For instance, fear might be used to motivate someone to stop smoking due to the cancer risks. That would be an appropriate use of an emotional appeal to support a logical argument about the cancer risks associated with smoking. However, arguing that capital punishment should be used to prevent the possibility of your grandmother being murdered is an illogical use of an emotional appeal since the chances of that one person being murdered if capital punishment were abolished is not likely. Emotional appeals should supplement logical arguments; emotional appeals alone often result in logical fallacies.

When considering how to use these appeals together, it might help to compare the persuasive appeal of an argument to a jury trial. The audience is the jury and each writer is a lawyer. Just as each lawyer presents a different logical explanation of the crime, puts forth evidence and witnesses, and uses emotions in opening and closing statements, the writer presents a logical argument, uses credible research as evidence, and might provide emotional appeals in introduction and conclusion paragraphs. After presenting an argument, the audience might not be totally convinced that you are right, but the audience should at least be convinced that you are a credible person with a logical argument.

To wrap up then, how can you make your argument most appealing to an academic or professional audience? Remember these key strategies:

- **Outline the logical argument by identifying its thesis and supporting reasons.** Identify the thesis by identifying the conclusion of the argument that the paper is proving to be true. List the supporting reasons and make sure that they make the thesis the logical result. Perhaps focus one paragraph on proving each reason to be true.

- **Avoid logical fallacies!**

- **Use good research to prove each reason to be true.** The research should be persuasive for the target audience. For instance, if writing an academic paper about strategies for overcoming depression, use articles published in scholarly journals read by professional psychologists (such as *The Journal of Clinical Psychology*) instead of articles about depression published in *USA Today* or on *WebMD*.

- **Proofread and edit carefully.** Credibility can be quickly lost, and can be difficult to recover, if there are many grammar, spelling, or formatting errors. Remember to edit carefully for precise word choice such as avoiding words like "all" or "none" if "most" or "few" are more accurate.

READING CRITICALLY

During lesson two, you read about the importance of seeking academic sources in writing. You were told to search for sources written by authoritative authors, who write without bias (favoring a particular side without a rational and justifiable reason). Using academic sources and experts can help strengthen your writing, not only in this course, but in your future work as well. This section of the course will discuss how to read these academic sources in a critical and analytic manner.

Often, college students approach written works as they would a biology or math textbook. They passively read the information and take the information at its surface value. However, when researching, it is important to get beneath the surface of a work, become an active reader, and understand the work at a deeper level.

To be able to examine a work critically, you must understand that work. However, sometimes you will encounter works that are quite tricky, especially peer-reviewed essays. This sort of difficulty occurs because peer-reviewed articles present researched information about a topic and do not necessarily give quick bites of information, as we often see in newspapers. If you choose to use journal articles when researching, it is helpful to print up the work. Then, as you are working through the article, use annotations off to the side after each paragraph. These annotations can briefly summarize each of these paragraphs and help you understand the essay as a whole. Be sure to define any technical jargon: words that are specifically related to a certain specialized field or discipline. You may also want to write these definitions off to the side. Then, when you have completed reading the article, review your side annotations.

After you understand the article and are able to summarize it, think about why an author wrote the essay. You must decide what the author's motive is behind the work. Is the author simply listing information to the reader, or does the author want to persuade the reader to believe a certain way or feel a certain emotion about an issue? Then, go further. How does the author work to influence the reader to believe or feel a certain way? Does this author use facts (logos)? Is the author an expert in the field (ethos)? Does the author try to make the reader feel a certain way through narration (pathos)? Are there argumentative

fallacies that affect or hinder this author's point? When you read a work critically, you not

only think about "what" the essay says, you also must think about "why" the author wrote

the essay and "how" the author tries to prove his/her point (thesis statement).

Here's an illustration. Please click on the following link: "In Japan, Nice Guys (and

Girls) Finish Together." Please note that you will have to enter your APUS login information.

To summarize the article, Nicholas D. Kristof discusses his experiences with Japanese

children at his son's birthday party in 1998. He explains that the Japanese children were

having difficulty playing some of the more competitive games at the party. Kristof then

states the following thesis statement: "American kids are taught to be winners, to seize their

opportunities and maybe the next kid's as well. Japanese children are taught to be good

citizens, to be team players, to obey rules, to be content to be a mosaic tile in some larger

design." He emphasizes this thesis with this: "The social and economic basis of modern

Japan is egalitarianism, and that does not leave much room for either winners or losers. In

Japan, winning isn't everything, and it isn't the only thing; in elementary schools it isn't even

a thing at all." Kristof attempts to prove his thesis through four additional case studies—a

discussion of his child's sports day at a Japanese kindergarten, his experience with

Japanese book reviewers, a personal interview with a Tokyo bank executive, and his wife's

birthing experience at a Japanese hospital. Basically, Kristof uses personal case studies

(pathos) to prove his point.

Would this article work as research for an argumentative essay? The year, of course,

would be the main issue. It is an older work (1998). However, let's say that you were tasked

with researching Japanese children at the end of 20th century. Would this article work for

that topic? Upon the initial reading, the article appears to make a compelling case. The author writes in an intelligent manner and has clearly lived in Japan. Also, this article was published in a reputable newspaper: *The New York Times*. Now, think critically about the work. Why did Kristof write this essay? He wants to prove to the reader that Japanese school children are less competitive than American children. How does Kristof prove this? He does not use statistics, conduct social experiments, or consult sociologists. He writes an expository essay using a personal narrative. Usually, what will sway an audience will be facts, statistics, and experts. Personal narratives can be useful in isolation to add pathos to an essay. However, a work that focuses on personal narratives would not be a strong source in an academic research essay because the facts that an article like this presents has not been proven. Relying on articles like the example above to prove points within your research paper could possibly weaken your argument. This is why it is important to approach works with a critical eye when conducting research.

Now, take a critical look at another essay. Please click on the following link: "Globalization and Education in Japan." You will have to enter your APUS login information in order to read this article by Kentaro Ohkura and Masako Shibata. When you open this article, you will notice right away that this article appears to be denser than Kristof's. This is where reading actively becomes even more essential and taking notations, as explained above, may be necessary.

Essentially, Ohkura and Shibata's essay focuses on a similar theme as Kristof's: Japan and education. Like Kristof, the authors write in an intelligent manner and appear to be quite knowledgeable about the subject. The source is reputable as well: *Yearbook Of The National Society For The Study Of Education*. Now, think critically. Why did the authors write this article? The authors attempt to prove the following point: Japan's educational position in the world has risen. They begin to prove this point by discussing the historical background of

Japanese education. Then, the authors discuss how Japan has adjusted its educational system in light of globalization: "including an educational system open to the masses, by adopting the American way of schooling as well as the system of liberal democracy" (Ohkura and Shibata 169). The authors also explain how the Japanese educational system focuses on "individual self-responsibility" (170). The authors use past history to prove their view (logos) and authoritative research to back up their points (ethos). Because these authors vary their methods of support and provide concrete evidence to back up their claim, the information provided within this essay could potentially be a valuable addition to a research paper.

As shown above, using critical thinking when researching can improve the quality of your written work. By thinking critically about how a work proves its argument, and not merely skimming through and passively summarizing the work, you will be better able to recognize strong sources. Using strong sources, of course, will help improve your written arguments.

Learning how to read critically will also help you with the critical evaluation essay as well. When you approach the essay you plan to discuss, make sure to think about why the author wrote this argument and how the author supports the argument. Do not fall into the trap of passively reading your chosen essay for information. Be an active reader and writer. Take your time to break down the article, and think about how each part works to prove the author's point. If a piece does not work, think about what the argumentative fallacy could be.

REVISING YOUR WORK

Reading critically will not only help you in understanding other essays, reading critically will also help you with your writing, especially when it comes to reviewing and revising your work. Passively reading your essay, and editing a word here and there, is simply the fine tuning. It is similar to frosting a cake that is not fully baked. Many students make the mistakes of getting bogged down with smaller technical issues (a comma splice, an incorrect use of a semi-colon), and they do not think about the effectiveness of the essay as a whole. When revising, there are actual steps that you can take in order to help your writing improve. Before you search for comma splices and run-on sentences, make sure that the content in your essay is as strong as it can be, that you have answered the assignment question, and that you have proven your thesis statement.

Mark Christenson speaks to the importance of revision in his article "The Importance of Revision in Writing Composition." Christenson states that when revising their own work, students not only learn how to become better writers. An honest appraisal of their own work will also help students learn more about their writing abilities, which will allow them to become more confident as writers. You can read more of his revision discussion by clicking on the following link and entering your APUS login information: "The Importance of Revision in Writing Composition." You may want to read through this article to discover more about why you should to revise your work.

Blum, Keller, and Tracy, in their essay "Commentary: Do Not Edit When You Need to Revise," discuss the differences of editing small technical issues and conducting a full revision of a work. They explain why students should revise a work prior to editing a work. Using word processing programs allows students to "produce a document with a clean and professional appearance." However, this clean appearance masks content issues that might occur once the reader actually reads the essay. These content issues should be revised, prior to the editing and formatting process. To read more about the differences between revision and editing, as presented by these authors in this article, please click on the following link: "Commentary: Do Not Edit When You Need to Revise."

When beginning your revision, be sure to read through the assignment in its entirety. Then, read through your essay. Make sure that you actually completed the assignment correctly. Often, students become focused on writing the essay and forget to actually complete the assignment properly (making sure to answer the assignment question, having the adequate number of sources, keeping the appropriate focus). You must verify that you have completed all the components of the assignment in your essay.

Next, check your thesis statement, and read it again. Make sure that your thesis statement not only has a topic, but that it also has a point (a claim). Sometimes students write thesis statements that state the topic of their research, but neglect to state what they plan to prove about this topic. Be sure that your thesis has both components. Remember that you are not writing a mystery novel. Reveal your exact point and claim within your thesis statement. The reader should know exactly what you plan to prove after completing your opening paragraph. Also, make sure your thesis statement is in fact a statement and not a question. The thesis statement should be the single, summary answer to your research question, not the original question itself. Finally, make sure that this thesis statement is at the bottom of your opening paragraph. At times, students try to place their thesis statement at the beginning of the introduction. However, when this is done, it can be tricky to continue the introduction. For example, some students who begin their essay with their thesis will continue the introduction by discussing specific points too early. Specific information like this is best left for the body of an essay.

After checking your thesis statement, read through each paragraph and make sure that the points presented in each paragraph work toward proving your thesis statement. If you find a paragraph that goes in another direction, you either need to remove that paragraph or rework your thesis, in light of what you have actually discussed in your essay. Do this with each body paragraph. Once you have decided that each paragraph works to prove your thesis statement, think about how you have organized these paragraphs. Is your essay organized in a logical manner? Does your essay transition properly from one paragraph to another? You may want to consider adding transitional phrases at the start of your paragraphs. This will help the reader to understand the connection between your thoughts, linking them in a seamless, coherent, and logical manner. Finally, sometimes it helps to arrange your paragraphs in order to end the body portion of your essay with your strongest body paragraph. This will ensure that your readers have the strongest persuasive point in mind as they conclude your essay.

After you have organized your essay, take a look at the length of each paragraph in relation to the other. Are the paragraphs around the same size? That is, make sure that you do not have several shorter paragraphs and several longer paragraphs. Each paragraph should be around (not exactly, though) the same length. This will ensure your points are presented, more or less, evenly. Additionally, make sure you have a thorough introduction and conclusion.

Once you have worked to organize your ideas as a whole, conduct a more detailed review of each individual paragraph. Does the paragraph start with a topic sentence that speaks to the overall point of the paragraph? Does each paragraph discuss one topic, and does not shift topics midway through? Do you discuss the information presented in this paragraph in a bias-free manner? If not, you must adjust your discussion. Also, make sure to define all technical jargon as well (but there is no need to define well-known terms). Check that the paragraph ends with your thoughts and not with a quotation. Be sure to check all of your references, and back-up any specific points with an in-text citation.

Only after you have examined your assignment details, your thesis, and your essay's structure, should you begin editing by delving into the smaller technical issues with the grammar and the citation format. To help catch smaller technical errors, it is important to read each sentence in isolation from the others. Some writers find it helpful to read the essay from the bottom up. Start by reading the final sentence out loud to yourself. Then, move on to the second to last sentence and so on. Remember, to remove the first and second person references (no I, you, me, and so on). When writing formal academic essays, it is best to use third person. Make sure to review the MLA citation information as presented in the second lesson. When in doubt, always consult MLA documentation sites regarding the format of a citation.

In a nutshell, when you revise your work, you should check for the following:

1. Check to make sure you have actually completed the assignment.

2. Check your thesis statement. It should have a topic, have a point, and be the final sentence of your opening paragraph.

3. Check to make sure that each paragraph works to prove the thesis. If a paragraph does not prove your thesis, remove it or adjust your thesis.

4. Check the organization of your essay and the size of your paragraphs.

5. Check that each paragraph focuses on one topic, and all information is cited correctly.

6. Check your grammar and the format of your citations.

In addition to revising and editing your work, find a proofreader. Do not be afraid to share your writing. Your proofreader may suggest ideas with which you disagree. That's fine. You do not have to take advantage of every suggestion. Almost invariably, however, your proofreader will discover an error of which you were unaware or make a suggestion that you had not considered. This is to be expected and is an important final step in the writing process.

INTRODUCTIONS

Earlier in this lesson, you learned about the importance of being able to read critically. Those critical reading skills are called into play the moment you begin to read the first paragraph of a piece. Without even being aware you make judgments about the article you are reading, as well as about its author. You decide if you like or trust or respect the author. You decide if this piece of writing is one you will continue to read and remember or one that you will put aside. In this process, you recognize the importance of the saying "You don't have a second chance to make a first impression."

That is why introductions are so important. A good introduction creates a first impression, one that invites the reader to continue into the work, or one that discourages the reader from proceeding. A good introduction is often described as a "hook," a tool used to reach and hold the reader's interest. It is also described as a doorway, an entry into the author's world, a place where the reader may learn new information, enjoy a positive literary experience, or possibly decide to pursue a specific course of action.

Given the importance of the introduction, it is a good idea for you to take great care in its construction. Many students find the introduction very difficult to do and some writing instructors encourage students to write the introduction after other parts of the essay have been completed. Guidelines offered in this lesson will help you take on the critical task of building a solid introduction that gets your readers inside your work.

One of the important things you should do before you begin your introduction is to ensure that you have enough knowledge about your topic to write confidently about it. Students often struggle with a writing assignment simply because they do not possess enough detailed information about the topic to move beyond making general statements. Specificity is a sign of a good writer and that results from a broad and deep understanding of the topic. Making sure that you are comfortable with your topic before you begin is a wise first step. One good way to do this is to have a conversation with someone about the topic. Often discussing the topic will help you see unanswered questions, holes in data, jumps in logic, and information that isn't closely related to your topic.

Once you feel comfortable with your level of knowledge about the topic, you can begin to decide how you want to open the door for your reader. Take time to understand who your intended audience is, so that your introduction will most effectively meet the reader's expectations. Ask yourself what the reader knows about your topic. Decide how much explanation you will need to provide initially to get your reader engaged. Ask yourself what the reader's attitude toward the topic looks like. Is the reader neutral, supportive of or opposed to your topic? Is your topic emotionally charged, one that has proponents and opponents lined up firmly and vehemently? Arguments about issues such as gun control and abortion are difficult to develop effectively because both sides have such strong and widely disseminated views. If your topic and stance are quite controversial, you will want to make sure that your introduction sets the stage for calm, rationale discourse.

After you have decided what your intended audience knows and feels about your topic and stance, you can begin to decide how to build your introduction. There are a number of tested strategies for getting a reader into your argument. It's helpful to look at examples.

To see one good introduction, click on the following link: <u>"The Struggle for Human Rights,"</u> delivered by Eleanor Roosevelt on September 28, 1948, in Paris, France.

Look carefully at this first paragraph. What techniques does Roosevelt use to get your interest, to invite you to hear her argument? What effect does she have on you by making an announcement of her topic, the preservation of human freedom, in the first sentence? How do you respond to the very simple language of the first sentence? What phrase does she repeat three times in this introductory paragraph? Why do you think she repeats this phrase? How is each use of the phrase different? Notice how she uses hyphens to set off three key words associated with the French Revolution (liberty, equality and fraternity). What is the impact of her announcing those three important nouns and then stating them? How do you respond to her pairing of the words freedom and tyranny? As you read through the entire speech, identify the points she makes to support her topic and stance. Does her introduction prepare you for what follows?

Roosevelt's simple language, use of repetition, and provision of vivid detailed reminders of recent events present a strong argument, one we are able to enter with ease because of her solid introduction.

As you read different arguments this semester, you will find a variety of introductory strategies. One effective kind of introduction involves the use of a pithy quotation. Using a sharp, brief statement, often made by a famous person, gets the reader's attention and initiates the relationship with the topic.

One example of an introduction that uses a quotation can be found by clicking on the APUS Library. Find the book *Closing Arguments: Clarence Darrow on Religion, Law, and*

Society, published by the Ohio University Press in 2005. Go to chapter 3 "On Politics and Society," and find the essay "Patriotism," beginning on page 175.

The author, Clarence Darrow, was one of the most important and well known defense attorneys in American history. Among the famous cases he defended was the Scopes monkey trial, about a teacher in Tennessee teaching the concept of evolution. The quotation Darrow selected to begin his essay on patriotism is from the writings of German philosopher Johann Wolfgang von Goethe (1749-1832) who, in addition to serving in his country's government, was also a novelist, dramatist, and scientist. Darrow published the essay in 1910, arguing for a movement away from narrow nationalism to the recognition that we are all connected in artistic, scientific, and moral pursuits.

Carefully read Goethe's quotation. What key point or points do you take from it? Do you agree with Goethe that art and science belong to the whole world? Do you accept Goethe's stance that art and science can only be promoted through open exchange and sharing past knowledge? After you have read Darrow's piece, answer these questions. How does the Darrow use Goethe's quotation as a springboard to his topic and stance? What specific strategies does he use to tie the quotation together with his own work? Would the essay be weaker if the quotation were omitted?

Quotations on various topics are easy to find. Visit the Summon search engine in the APUS Library. You will be asked to log in. Once you have logged in, type "quotations" in the Search box. You do not have to have quote marks around the word. Click "Book/eBook" on the left side to see a list of quotation resources in library. Select one of these sources. Examine its table of contents and browse through the work. Try finding a topic you like, either through the table of contents or index in the volume. If you can't think of a topic, try one of these: loyalty, perseverance, sunrise, or memory. Then explore the quotations listed for that topic.

Think about what kind of argument essay you might write using one of the quotations as part of your introduction. Identify ways this quotation might support a stance you would take on the topic. Practice with a few quotations until you become comfortable with the process. Remember that after you find a quotation you like, it's a good idea to gather information about the author so you can put the quotation in context. If you use a quotation in your essay, you must cite it properly.

Another commonly used and powerful entry is to begin an essay with an anecdote, which is a brief story. This approach is effective because we love storytelling. Cultures have long passed on important information from one generation to another through stories or fables or parables. You can probably remember accounts your parents told you as you were growing up about children who ended up in trouble or were hurt because they did forbidden things like playing with matches or taking candy from strangers. Storytelling is something we like to do.

In an argument essay, an anecdote can quickly engage the reader. Descriptive details and smooth narration of events can create a powerful word picture for the reader. From there the author can merge the story with the essay's thesis statement and move into the body of the essay, knowing that the reader is already connected to the writer's position.

A powerful introduction using anecdote can be seen in Eric Zorn's blog post, "Death Penalty and Deterrence—the Argument from Anecdote," published in the *Chicago Tribune* on April 23, 2011. The post appeared after the governor of Illinois abolished the death penalty in the state.

What impacts do the introductory sentences have on you? Does the author get your interest? Is he successful in engaging you with his argument? How does Zorn's introductory account of a crime connect with his stance that the risk of executing an innocent person far outweighs the death penalty's deterrence of future crimes? Would the post be as effective if the anecdote were omitted?

This blog post is especially appropriate for this section of the lesson because it speaks to the use of anecdotes in building an argument. Zorn says that data should rate higher than anecdotes when making public policy decisions such as the use of the death penalty. While the author makes a good point about the problem of using anecdotes as proof in an argument, he does in fact use the tool effectively to get the reader into his work.

There are other good ways to get your reader into your argument essay, including using intriguing statistics and asking rhetorical questions. Statistics, especially if they are surprising or impressive, can intrigue the reader and set the stage for the stance you will take. For example, this astounding statistic, taken from the Humane Society of the United States, could provide a powerful entry into an argument essay about the importance of spaying and neutering pets: "About 2.7 million cats and dogs—about one every eleven seconds—are put down in U.S. shelters each year." The introductory paragraph could describe how long it would typically take to read the essay and how many animals would have been put down during that time. This rousing account could lead nicely into a reasoned discussion of the importance of spaying and neutering pets.

Rhetorical questions are another way of engaging the reader right away. These are devices authors include to rouse curiosity. An answer is not really expected. Rhetorical questions are common in discourse and run the gamut from the popular and much copied advertising copy "Got milk?" to Shylock's famous lines from Shakespeare's *Merchant of Venice*:

> Hath not a Jew eyes?
>
> Hath not a Jew hands, organs, dimensions, senses, affections, passions?
>
> If you prick us, do we not bleed, if you tickle us, do we not laugh?
>
> If you poison us, do we not die?

When we read a rhetorical question (such as "How often do you blink in an hour?") we tend to try to formulate an answer. For example, it is likely that you may have just estimated how many times you blink in an hour. When we read rhetorical questions, we become involved in the issue almost involuntarily.

To see an illustration of an effective introduction using a rhetorical question, click on the following link: "The Real Language Crisis," by Russell Berman, published in *Academe 97.5*, September/October 2011.

Russell Berman's argument, that higher education needs to more strongly emphasize the acquisition of second-languages to prevent American from being isolated from other nations, is introduced effectively through the use of a rhetorical question. Berman asks if higher education in America will provide the chance to understand others across the globe or will it collapse, in response to "isolationism and xenophobia." Xenophobia is an unreasonable fear of strangers, foreigners, or those different from ourselves.

Berman asks the reader to think about these two poles: listening to voices around the world or isolating ourselves in fear. How do you respond to his question? What kinds of possible responses form in your mind? Do you find yourself leaning toward one choice? Does the question effectively set the stage for the rest of Berman's argument? Would removing the rhetorical question weaken his introduction?

There are other strategies that work well in introductions. Sometimes simply jumping in to your topic is the best way to get started. Sometimes it is a good idea to explain right away why a reader should care about your topic. Other times it is effective to provide a brief history of a topic in your introduction, providing background information for the reader.

Whatever strategy you decide to use in your introduction, you will want the introduction to create context for the topic and encourage the reader to feel the need to read more about the topic. You will do this in your introduction, in part, with your thesis statement.

As you build your introduction for the argument essay, it is recommended that you state your thesis statement clearly and include in that thesis both your topic and the stance you are going to take. This is explained in more detail below in the section on thesis statements. It is also recommended that your thesis statement be located at the end of your introduction. This allows you time to provide your reader some background information about the topic and to establish your credibility to write on this topic. Locating your thesis at the end of your introduction helps ensure that you will not begin to provide the detailed evidence to support your stance too soon, that you will save it for the body paragraphs that follow.

In a nutshell, you should keep these things in mind when writing your introduction:

1. You should have a solid understanding of your topic so you can confidently discuss it in detail.

2. You should build your introduction so it "hooks" the reader's attention and invites the reader to continue into your essay.

3. You should use an introduction that is appropriate for your topic and audience.

4. You can choose from a number of approaches, including the use of quotation, anecdote, statistics, rhetorical question, background information, and a brief description of the topic and stance.

5. You should put your thesis statement at the end of your introduction, so it can smoothly guide your reader into the body of your argument.

THESIS STATEMENTS

Earlier in this lesson, in the section on revising your work, you were given guidance on the thesis statement. A thesis statement is a critical element of your essay, in that it is the core of your piece. It is what the essay is all about. It is more, however, than just an announcement of your main idea. A helpful way to think of a thesis statement is to visualize it as the hub of a spoked wheel. It hooks everything together. All paragraphs span out from this center; the essay rolls smoothly with the thesis as its hub. The thesis statement should be strong enough to hold the body paragraphs together.

The thesis statement needs to have two key elements: a topic and a point (a stance). It isn't enough to say that you will discuss the reintroduction of wolves in the western United States. You must also include in the thesis statement what your point will be about that reintroduction. You may include descriptive details about the reasons, process and results of reintroduction, but you should, in an argument essay, also have a point to prove. Your point may be that the reasons for its introduction were not based on sound evidence; your point may be that the process used for its reintroduction omitted key stakeholders; your point may be that the results of its reintroduction have been devastating to certain resources or citizens. You want to include both key elements, a topic and a point, in your thesis statement.

A good thesis statement is written as one complete sentence. It should not be a question. Frequently, when a student couches her thesis statement as a question, her actual thesis statement may be the answer to that question. For example, a student may say that this is her thesis statement: "Shouldn't American parents demand that toy packaging be ecologically friendly?" If her essay goes on to demonstrate the environmental impacts of toy packaging and the ease with which such a change in packaging could be made, her actual thesis statement may in fact be "American parents should demand that toy packaging, which contributes significantly to environmental degradation, be ecologically friendly, a change that would have minimal impacts on toymakers' profits."

It is a good idea to avoid phrasing your thesis statement as a compound (that is, two-part) sentence. Doing so often sends you, and therefore the reader, in two different directions. Here is an example of a proposed thesis statement, formatted as a compound sentence. "Uniforms should be required for all public middle school students and the clothing selected should be made in the United States of materials produced in this country." Does the writer want to address the issue of uniforms as a way of improving learning conditions for middle school students or does the writer want to argue for providing business for American producers and manufacturers? The thesis statement seems to convey that its author is going to try to prove two different points. You should try to avoid this kind of two-pronged approach. Try to keep your thesis statement a clear, focused, simple declarative sentence. Work to ensure that your reader knows exactly what your topic is and what you are going to prove about that topic.

Some students use general, sweeping statements as their thesis statements, a strategy that is not often successful. Examples of such generalizations might be "For centuries war has inflicted horrors on countries" or "Humans have suffered immensely because of intense storms" or "Domestic abuse should be eliminated as it has become a serious problem in our nation." It is much better to drill down into more specific detail for a powerful thesis statement.

Other students build their thesis statements around a dictionary's definition of a term. An example of this kind of thesis is "The *Merriam Webster's Dictionary* defines 'discrimination' as 'a prejudiced or prejudicial outlook, action, or treatment' and that accurately describes the kind of unfair treatment the homeless are currently experiencing in our community." A definition can serve as a springboard for a good argument, particularly if the writer is going to provide solid evidence that sheds new light on a commonly accepted definition. In addition, definitions of terms that may be unknown to the reader are critical in some argument essays. But using a dictionary definition as the basis for your thesis statement is not recommended.

Where is the best place to put a thesis statement? As indicated earlier, the preferred location for a thesis statement in an argument essay is at the end of the first paragraph. Beginning the paragraph with your thesis often leads to providing multiple details of support in that first paragraph, details that you will actually be covering more fully in subsequent body paragraphs.

Should a thesis statement ever be invisible, that is, implied? Some writers can accomplish their goals by having an implied thesis statement, one that is not specifically spelled out, but one that forms in the reader's mind, a result of carefully constructed logic and abundant detail. However, in the type of argument essays you are writing in this class and will typically write in other academic and professional settings, it is advisable to specifically state your thesis. Leave no doubt in the reader's mind what your topic is and what stance you are taking.

Should a thesis statement ever be located at the end of an essay? Some writers can put their thesis statements at the end of an essay, often following a build-up of vivid details, delivering a powerful final punch to the work. Like an implied thesis statement, a thesis statement at the end of an essay may not be the most appropriate and effective choice for the essays you will be doing in your college and career writing, particularly in argument essays.

In summary, you should keep these things in mind when writing your thesis statement:

1. Your thesis statement is the core of the essay.

2. You should include two elements in your thesis statement: the topic and your point (stance).

3. The thesis statement should be a single, declarative sentence, not a question.

4. You should avoid using broad generalizations or dictionary definitions as thesis statements.

5. You should put your thesis statement at the end of your introduction, so it can smoothly guide your reader into the body of your argument.

WRITING CONCLUSIONS

Writing a good conclusion is as important a task as writing a good introduction. This is your last chance to connect with the reader, to have your final bit of conversation together. Readers will take a memorable conclusion with them, possibly carrying that bit of prose long after the essay was read.

You don't get a second chance to make a first impression and you only have one chance to make a lasting impression as you finish your essay. Carefully planning and constructing your conclusion so that it reinforces your thesis statement is critical.

It will be important that your conclusion has a sense of finality to it. The reader needs to know that you are finished, that you've said what you have to say. You don't want to leave the reader hanging, wondering "Is there a final page missing?" Some teachers may suggest that, to create this sense of finality, you end by taking your reader back to where you started. That approach can be effective. It can also seem a bit contrived, so if you use this circular movement, do so carefully. Give your reader a fresh view, not just a reiteration of the information you presented at the beginning.

Readers like a sense of completion. They like the feel of having worked through an argument with the author, reaching a satisfying end to the trek. It's much like the feeling one may have after reading a good mystery or watching a high quality movie. Things make sense; ends are tied up neatly; the ending feels just right.

What are some good ways to end your argument essay? Not surprisingly many of these ways are similar to methods used for introductions. Anecdotes, quotations and statistics could be used effectively to wrap up your argument, as could rhetorical questions. The guidance set forth about these items in the section of the lesson about introductions would also apply to their use in conclusions.

You may want to use the conclusion to summarize your key points, but don't just stop there. It's a good idea to synthesize, rather than summarize. Give your reader something more than just a repetition of assertions you made earlier. What does it mean to synthesize information? To understand the term, it's helpful to think about what you do when you analyze something: you break it down into component parts. When you synthesize information, you do almost the opposite. Instead of breaking something down into parts, you put parts together to create something new. You combine pieces of information, pieces that are often dissimilar from each other, and you meld them into a coherent whole. When you think about a synthesizer in a musical sound system, you think about a piece of equipment that merges differing tones to make a pleasing bit of music. That is what you do when you provide synthesis at the end of your argument. You help the reader see the disparate pieces of information that you provided as a unified, satisfying bit of discourse.

Many good writers use the conclusion of an argument to challenge the reader, maybe to make the reader move out of a comfort zone. This challenge may take the form of thinking differently about a topic or it may take the form of a call to action. The argument may be so persuasive that the reader will, in fact, follow directions in the conclusion to contact public officials or to change personal habits of resource consumption.

It may be effective for a writer to issue a warning to the reader, a cautionary projection about what consequences may occur if action is not taken. Such a warning should be issued in an understated, calm way. A reader would not want to feel that "the sky is falling!" after reading your argument.

Projecting your reader into the future, into the possible consequences of a situation that is not changed, is a way to help the reader answer the "So what?" question about an argument. You should, throughout your argument, be providing detailed evidence about why this issue should matter to the reader. You should be stressing the importance of your topic and stance through the body of your essay. Your conclusion is one more opportunity to tell your reader how important this issue is. This is your final chance to make a lasting mark in your reader's memory, something she will carry with her after she has finished reading your work.

To summarize, these are points you should keep in mind when writing your conclusion:

1. Your conclusion needs to create a sense of completion.

2. Techniques like anecdotes, quotations, statistics, and rhetorical questions work well for conclusions.

3. You should synthesize, that is pull together, rather than just summarize points you have presented.

4. You may want to set forth possible consequences of the situation you have been exploring. This may even take the form of a warning.

5. You may challenge the reader or make a call to action.

6. Your conclusion should answer the "So what?" question, convincing the reader of the importance of your topic and stance.

7. You should avoid weaker endings, such as broad general statements.

8. You should leave a final vivid impression on your reader.

CONCLUSION

This completes lesson three. This is a longer lesson; however, make sure to fully understand the concepts that were explained to you, for the material presented in this lesson will help you create stronger arguments. Next time you read an essay (including your own work), consider how the author opened the essay and the author's thesis statement. Also, think about the persuasive appeals that author used (if any) and if the author committed any argumentative fallacies. Did the author effectively revise the argument, and did that author conclude in a thoughtful manner? Approaching written arguments in an active, critical manner will help improve your writing and reading skills.

QUESTIONS TO CONSIDER

1. How can utilizing the persuasive appeals improve your arguments?

2. What argumentative errors should you be aware of when researching a topic?

3. How can reading critically improve your writing?

4. Why is it important to revise a work before editing it?

5. What are some of the components of an effective introduction and conclusion?

Works Cited

Berman, Russell. "The Real Language Crisis." *Academe 97.5.* Sept./Oct. 2011: 30-34.

    ProQuest. Web. 1 Jan. 2012.

Blum, E. Joan , M. Martin, E. Keller, and J. Tracy. "Commentary: Do Not Edit When You Need

    To Revise." *Rhode Island Lawyers Weekly* (n.d.): Regional Business News. Web. 26

    Nov. 2011.

Christiansen, Mark. "The Importance Of Revision In Writing Composition." *Education Digest*

    56.2 (1990): 70-72. *Academic Search Premier.* Web. 26 Nov. 2011.

Darrow, Clarence. "Patriotism." *Closing Arguments: Clarence Darrow on Religion, Law, and*

    Society. Athens, OH, USA: Ohio University Press, 2005. 183. Web. 1 Jan 2012.

Humane Society of the United States. *Pet Overpopulation.* Web. 1 Jan. 2012.

Kristof, Nicholas D. "Correspondence/Uncompetitive in Tokyo; In Japan, Nice Guys (And

    Girls) Finish Together." *New York Times* 12 Apr. 1998: 7. *Academic Search Premier.*

    Web. 25 Nov. 2011.

Lucas, Stephen E. "The Stylistic Artistry of the Declaration of Independence." *National*

    Archives, 1989. Web. 4 Dec. 2011

    <http://www.archives.gov/exhibits/charters/declaration_style.html>.

Ohkura, Kentaro, and Masako Shibata. "Globalization And Education In Japan." *Yearbook Of*

    The National Society For The Study Of Education (Wiley-Blackwell) 108.2 (2009):

    160-179. *Education Research Complete.* Web. 25 Nov. 2011.

Roosevelt, Eleanor. "The Struggle for Human Rights." Paris, France. 28 Sept. 1948. Web. 1

    Jan. 2012.

Zorn, Eric. "Death Penalty and Deterrence---the Argument from Anecdote." *Change of*

    Subject. Chicago Tribune. 23 Apr. 2011. Web. 1 Jan. 2012.

CHAPTER 4: NEGOTIATING THE OPPOSITION AND USING THE TOULMIN METHOD OF ARGUMENTATION

INTRODUCTION

Lesson four emphasizes looking at an argument critically, responding to opposing views in a way that helps strengthen your argument, and getting ready to write an argument based on the Toulmin model. Thinking about your experience, both in writing and speech, will help you identify effective ways to argue, as well as those techniques you typically use. Assessing and responding to opponents will be covered, including steps you can take to increase your credibility with those who disagree with you. The process of "negotiating" with the opposition will be explored, providing you strategies that will help strengthen your argument. The Toulmin model for argument will be covered in this lesson, giving you an effective way to assess opposing views, as well as setting the groundwork for the Toulmin-based argument you will write in the next lesson. Lesson four will conclude with guidance about selecting your topic for the Toulmin argument.

ARGUMENTS YOU HAVE ENCOUNTERED

When we think about arguments, we typically have memory flashes of unpleasant confrontations in the past, where we have encountered opposition to our own views and may have been challenged about them. We often try to push those memories of arguments behind us. But as we are developing skills in writing arguments, it is important that we examine how we respond to someone whose view is different from our own.

Delving into this lesson, you have been encouraged to think about how you have dealt with opposing viewpoints in the past. As you considered that question, did certain memories come up? Did you recall a family dinner that became tense because opposing viewpoints were set forth in less than cordial terms? Were there situations with other students that resulted in hostile declarations of two polarities? Or did you encounter situations where differing views were treated with respect? If you could recall a very civil disagreement, what made that situation stand out in your mind? What did each side do to maintain an air of courtesy and respect?

When you write an argument, you should aim to create a sense of civility, one in which an opposing view, while it may be very different from your own, would still be respected. It is very easy to see examples of contentious arguments. Television, talk radio, blogs, and even athletic events provide numerous examples of arguments that are not conducted with civility and respect. This lesson will provide guidance on how to recognize and respond to opposing views in a way that recognizes the dignity and worth of the opponent.

You were also asked to look at the arguments you currently make, arguments that may be written or spoken (oral). As you looked at those arguments, did you determine that they had an identifiable structure? When you present a case orally, do you typically have a clear sense of the kinds of approaches you will take to convince your listener that your view should be accepted? For example, if you approach your supervisor with a proposal about changing a workplace procedure, do you have a defined way that you try to "sell" this idea? Do you make brief notes before you speak? Do you typically identify both the positive and negative consequences that may result from carrying out your plan? Do you typically try to anticipate what objections might occur?

Thinking about these examples is helpful as you work on your arguments. You can see where you have used sound principles of good argumentation and apply those principles to your writing.

RESPONDING TO AN OPPOSING VIEWPOINT

Thinking carefully about the way you typically argue is a helpful first step as you begin your work on writing arguments. Another important step is to recognize and respond appropriately to the person or persons representing a viewpoint that opposes your own.

One of the keys to presenting a successful argument is maintaining your credibility in the eyes of the reader. It is important to create and sustain the notion that you understand the topic and that you are fair, open-minded, and objective in your analysis of it. It is worthwhile to take the time to study and assess the viewpoint that opposes your own, as well as the characteristics of your opponent. You should learn enough about the opposing viewpoint that you are able to "negotiate" opposing arguments, thus strengthening your case and increasing your credibility with your audience. The act of negotiating maintains its focus on give-and-take rather than conquer. This important skill of negotiating opposition will help you, not only in this class, but in future college courses and your activities outside of the classroom.

DOING YOUR HOMEWORK

Negotiating opposition starts with learning about the opponent's viewpoint. It is very important to take the time to gather enough information about that viewpoint so that your comprehension is clearly visible. Showing a lack of understanding about an opposing viewpoint, demonstrating a failure to "do your homework," can weaken your credibility.

A fine example of someone who has studied carefully about opposing viewpoints is Congresswoman Shirley Anita St. Hill Chisholm who presented a speech to Congress on

August 10, 1970, concerning the Equal Rights Amendment. You can find this speech at the end of this lesson.

Congresswoman Chisholm begins her speech with a simple declaration that discrimination against women, based solely on gender, is so widespread that it may seem natural and acceptable. While she concedes that passage of the amendment will not remove prejudice from people's hearts, she says there is no reason to protect and revere this prejudice in our laws.

As you look through Chisholm's speech, identify the many spots where she demonstrates that she has "done her homework" about the opposing point of view. For example, she first discusses the constitutional right of due process. She shows her understanding of this broad right by citing examples as diverse as exclusion from university attendance or jury duty and application of criminal penalties. How does she address the opposing view that passage of the amendment would result in a state of "legal confusion" and much litigation? Does her response have credence with you?

Chisholm addresses point after point held by opponents. Note how she faces opposition related to economics, military service, labor laws, survivor benefits, alimony, and pay equity. Her brief speech is a comprehensive catalog of areas of American life impacted by gender discrimination. She clearly studied her opposition before speaking; Chisholm did her homework.

UNDERSTANDING THE COMPLEXITY OF THE OPPOSING VIEW

In addition to taking time to learn about your opponent, you should also make sure that you understand the complexity and nuances of the opposing viewpoint. Should you oversimplify the stance or minimize its impact, you create questions of doubt in the reader's mind.

You can see a solid example of someone who addresses a complex issue and the nuances that may be among opposing viewpoints by listening to the address President Gerald Ford gave to the nation on September 8, 1974, announcing that he was pardoning Richard M. Nixon: <u>President Gerald Ford's Address to the Nation.</u> You can also find his speech at the end of this lesson.

Notice how he presents himself to Americans in the first paragraph. What is the effect of his saying that the difficult decisions he has to make are different from the hypothetical questions that he has quickly responded to in the past? Why do you think he spends so much time discussing how he makes decisions? What forces are at work in his decision-making that may seem to be at odds with each other? What kinds of authority does he rely on in making his decision to pardon Richard Nixon? How does he explain these sources of authority to his listeners?

President Ford could have just exercised his authority as President of the United States, announced his decision to pardon, and cited legal rationale for his decision. How would that approach have differed from this one? Does it make sense to you that he addresses the complexities that are related to more issues than just the law?

RECOGNIZING THE EMOTIONAL ELEMENTS OF THE OPPOSITION

President Ford's pardon of Richard Nixon dealt with a very emotional issue and his speech specifically recognized that. In addition to communicating how complex the issue was, in order to sway his opponents, he also paid attention to the emotional elements of the issue. It is important in negotiating the opposition to recognize strong emotional elements that may be affecting the issue. Even though your argument may be relying primarily on logic and your credibility (logos and ethos) for its proof, you need to recognize and respect any strong emotions that may accompany the issue. You do not want to disregard pathos. For example, arguments about abortion and gun control typically have very strong emotional components and an effective argument on one of these topics would acknowledge and respect the readers' feelings about the topics.

Just as President Ford recognized and addressed the emotional facets as he presented his decision, so did US Attorney General Robert Kennedy include his listeners' and his own emotions in speaking about the assassination of Martin Luther King. Kennedy's remarks are poignant, in that his own brother had been assassinated. They are also significant because he subsequently lost his own life to an assassin's bullet. You can listen to these remarks by clicking on this link: Robert F. Kennedy's Remarks on the Assassination of Martin Luther King, Jr. You can also find his speech at the end of this lesson.

As you read through Kennedy's speech, you will most likely note how short it is and how it seems to be impromptu and unpolished. First he announces that Martin Luther King has been shot and killed. From there, look at the options he sets forth for African Americans. Look at the plea he makes for actions that models King's. Examine the way he seeks to show his empathy, the way he was presented with the options of hatred and mistrust following his brother's assassination. Kennedy sets forth a simple argument, a call to action following a great tragedy. The brevity, clarity and acknowledgement of opponents' likely emotional responses make these remarks an effective argument, even though they appear to be spontaneous and informal. They work because Kennedy recognized the emotional volatility of the issue and negotiated with the opposition in a compassionate, concise way.

ACKNOWLEDGING THE DIVERSITY OF OPPONENTS

In contrast with Kennedy's remarks is the speech given by Carrie Chapman Catt to Congress about women's suffrage (the right to vote). Catt's argument is very formal, polished, and directed at the views of her opponents. You can find Catt's speech at the end of this lesson.

Catt says three distinct causes make suffrage inevitable. What are those? Does her use of transitional words (first, second, third) strengthen her case? She follows these three strong points with a series of rhetorical questions. What effects do these questions have on you?

The final third of her presentation is directed specifically at the members of Congress. Note how she invites them to adopt suffrage as a party platform, to essentially join forces with the country's women and their supporters. She recognizes that Congressmen will meet opposition and provides counsel for them. Then she directly addresses categories of Congressmen: those who have already become supporters; those who have shown only casual interest in the topic; those who have served in Congress for a long time; and those who think that suffrage is a decision that should be addressed state by state. How do you respond to her suggestions for each of these groups? Do you think her argument is effective?

Although some may find Catt's approach a bit too direct, it is hard to deny that she reaches out to the diversity of opponents facing her. She knows them. She knows what their motives may be. She knows what "buttons to push" for each group. Her negotiation with opponents is comprehensive and personalized.

Each of these presentations demonstrates specific attention to the opposing viewpoint. Whether the presenter has chosen to thoroughly study the opposing view, carefully explain the complexities of opposition, recognize the emotions at work in the opponents' response to an issue, or address the diversity of opponents, the strategies are aimed at the same goal. All are designed to set the stage for a successful exchange with those who may not share the same point of view. All are designed to increase the chances that the argument presented will be ultimately met with acceptance.

SELECTING OPPOSING VIEWS

The Congressional presentation made by Carrie Chapman Catt demonstrated the speaker's attention to the diversity of her opposition. She explored an array of opponents whose views, while all in opposition to her stance, may differ from one to the next. Similarly, your exploration of opposing views may reveal a spectrum of opponents, ranging from weakly supported and illogical ones to those who have set forth clear reasons and abundant, appropriate evidence. It is important for you to address the strongest of your opponents, not just to challenge yourself, but also to make your argument withstand its most vigorous attack. While it may be easy to discount the views of a weak opponent, don't stop there. Take on the tough one. Demonstrate that you respect the good work a strong opponent has conducted in presenting this case.

SUMMARIZING THE OPPOSING VIEW

Once you have selected opponent(s) for your argument, you need to decide how you will share your knowledge of that opposing view with your reader. Often that sharing occurs in a single statement. But other times, a lengthier presentation of opposition is needed and that can be done by summarizing.

Summarizing an opponent's view is an effective way to help you understand the opposing stance, as well as to convey to the reader your understanding and objectivity. When you summarize the opposition you should ensure that you are accurate and understandable. Confusing your reader about the opponent will not serve you well. Aim for thoroughness as you set forth the opponent's view. Avoid simplification if it leaves out key aspects that would provide good support for the opposing stance. You should also ensure that your summary is neutral, that it does not appear to be biased or filled with "loaded" or antagonistic language. Be careful that the words you choose do not have connotations (emotional elements) that may reflect negatively on your opponent, even though the words' denotations (dictionary meanings) are applicable. Do not distort your opponent's view either explicitly or implicitly. Be above board. Be clear. Be thorough. Be accurate.

Here is a chance for you to compare two summaries of the same piece. To see the argument being reviewed, click on the following link: Dita Wickins-Drazilova's <u>"Zoo Animal</u> <u>Welfare."</u> Dr. Wickins-Drazilova has written a number of journal articles focusing on ethics applied to childhood, public health, biotechnology and animal and environmental issues.

After you have read her article, look over these two summaries. One is unfair, oversimplified, and biased. The other is clear, accurate, and fair.

Unfair Summary of "Zoo Animal Welfare" by Dita Wickins-Drazilova

In a piece that looks like a polished speech from a PETA (People for the Ethical Treatment of Animals) conference, Wickins-Drazilova laments the pitiable state of zoo animals. She creates melodramatic scenarios of pathetic creatures suffering poor physical health, living long past their "prime," and being forced to reproduce in unsavory settings, such as small cages or dark pits. Ignoring the animals' basic needs is not the only horror on Wickins-Drazilova's list. Zoo animals also suffer the loss of freedom and choice and dignity and the ability to act out in abnormal ways. The emotionally battered reader is led to believe that even pigs bred for slaughter live better lives than do animals in zoos. "Zoo Animal Welfare" is packed with sorrowful images that will bring tears to a sensitive reader's eyes and maybe even lead the reader to write out a check to PETA.

Fair Summary of "Zoo Animal Welfare" by Dita Wickins-Drazilova

In a thorough exploration of the well being of zoo animals, Dr. Wickins-Drazilova makes a strong case for re-examining the purpose and operation of zoos. Clearly stated, well-documented research is set forth, as the author traces the status of the most common measurements for zoo animals' welfare. These include physical health, longevity and reproduction. But she does not stop there, instead moving the assessment to key issues of freedom and choice, differences between normal and abnormal behaviors, and, most important, dignity. The author suggests that human as well as animal needs be weighed and that zoos be re-defined to encompass multiple purposes.

What words in the first summary are loaded? What elements in the first summary serve to trivialize Wickins-Drazilova's work? Conversely, what features of the second summary make it more neutral, and therefore appropriate, as part of an argument?

Providing an accurate, clear, thorough and neutral summary of an opponent's view is one important part of negotiating opposition. Another is challenging the opponent's stance, evidence, and underlying assumptions. To explore this approach further, it is helpful to examine the work of Stephen Toulmin.

TOULMIN ARGUMENT

Stephen Toulmin was a philosopher who determined that the format of classical argument was not always helpful. He felt it did not represent the arguments typically seen in oral and written discourse, nor did it help speakers and writers build effective arguments. He created a different approach, called the Toulmin argument, which provides tools for exploring how an argument is built and how well it is supported.

For a good overview of Toulmin's life and key work, please click on the following link: <u>"Stephen Toulmin, a Philosopher and Educator, Dies at 87."</u> As you read through this summary of his life and work, pay special attention to the discussion of his book *The Uses of Argument*, published in 1958, and of the Toulmin method set forth in that book. You will see that the Toulmin method is described as being very valuable for determining the strong and weak points of an argument, which is what we are going to address in this lesson. You will also note that the Toulmin method has been applied, not just in the realms of debate and writing, but in fields as diverse as computer science and literary criticism.

You will be spending some time in this class working with the Toulmin argument. At first it may seem a bit confusing, because it is different from the way most of us have learned to build an argument. Don't worry. As you read and work with the Toulmin method, you will be more comfortable. It is likely that you will find yourself applying the approach to claims you see around you, including those made at work, those in reading you do for other classes, or those in advertisements in print or electronic media.

Your first step is to learn Toulmin's terms. You can then apply them in negotiating opposition. Here are the terms used in the Toulmin method:

Claim: A claim is a statement that sets forth the writer's opinion on the topic, the stance the writer is taking, the point the writer is going to make. A claim may be called a proposition or a thesis, the single statement that connects all elements of the argument. A claim is the statement that the writer is asking the reader to accept as true. The claim must have support for the argument to be effective.

Support (also called Grounds or Data): Support is composed of evidence that a writer uses to prove the claim. Support is usually a combination of facts and reasoning. It may include statistics, data, expert testimony, interviews, observations, and persuasive appeals (logos, ethos, and pathos).

Qualifier: A writer who uses absolutes (typically associated with terms like these: *always, never, everyone, no one*) quickly loses credibility in the reader's mind, as situations are rarely absolute. So good writers use qualifiers to clarify their claims and maintain credibility by acknowledging that, though their claim might be true most of the time, it is not an absolute. Commonly used qualifiers are shown here: *usually, some, several, often, sometimes, typically, and for the most part.* Excessive use of qualifiers can weaken an argument.

Warrant: A warrant is an underlying assumption or inference that the writer takes for granted. It essentially sets up an agreement between the writer and reader that the issue at hand is an important one. Warrants are often based on values that the writer and reader share. They do not have to be specifically stated but can be implied. If a reader does not agree with the underlying assumption that the writer takes for granted, it is unlikely that the writer's claim will be accepted.

Backing: In instances where a warrant is not well known, understood or accepted, it may be necessary to have additional evidence to defend the warrant. This evidence is called the backing. It may take the same forms as the claim's support (statistics, facts, expert testimony, and so on).

Concession and Rebuttal: A concession is an acknowledgement by the writer that a part of the opposing argument is valid and cannot be refuted. By conceding on an opponent's point, the writer is enhancing his/her own credibility and offering a respectful outreach to the opponent. It is not necessary, as part of a concession, for the writer to give up or change the claim. Writers may decide to offer their opponents concessions to valid points, but they may also decide that points made by opponents are not ones they want to concede. They would then use rebuttals. A rebuttal is a counterargument that addresses an opponent's point, showing it to be invalid and refutable. The rebuttal can start the cycle of claim, support, warrant, concession and rebuttal on its own. As with concessions, a rebuttal can enhance the credibility of the writer, if done properly.

Stephen Toulmin's approach to argument offers writers a systematic way to test their claims by looking at specific kinds of evidence (support), at underlying assumptions and their evidence (warrants and backings), and at possible responses from opponents (concessions and rebuttals).

EXAMPLE OF TOULMIN-BASED ARGUMENT

Below is a simple argument the authors have crafted, showing the Toulmin elements described above. (Please note that this essay was created specifically for the purpose of demonstrating the Toulmin elements; the studies mentioned in it do not exist. In your paper, you will want, of course, to use actual studies and provide appropriate citation.)

No More Junk Food for Our Kids at School

Having junk food, defined as high calorie food with low nutritional value, available in public school vending machines should be banned because it contributes to the dangerous rise in children's obesity. Junk food availability at school prevents children from getting the nutrition they need for critical physical and mental development. A recent study released by the USDA showed that recommended nutritional levels of children in schools with junk food in vending machines were almost 30% lower than those in schools without. Surveys conducted at numerous school districts in the Pacific Northwest showed that, when given the opportunity, most children would spend funds given them to purchase nutritional cafeteria food on junk food in vending machines.

Having healthier children is something this country values. If junk food in public school vending machines is eliminated, we help improve the health of our children, which increases our prospects for sound, fit future citizens and reduces our nation's healthcare costs.

While it can be said that junk food in small amounts is not harmful to children's diets, it remains a fact that our children are alarmingly overweight and school vending machines provide convenient opportunities for consumption of harmful foods without proper parental supervision of food choices.

Vending machines have been identified as contributing significantly to revenue-strapped school districts and some feel that removing junk food from vending machines will reduce that revenue. Eliminating junk food from vending machines and replacing it with healthy foods will still provide school districts revenue and children higher quality, healthier foods.

Here is the same essay, with the Toulmin elements identified:

No More Junk Food for Our Kids at School

Having junk food, defined as high calorie food with low nutritional value, available in public school vending machines should be banned [**This is the Claim**] because it contributes to the dangerous rise in children's obesity [**This is the Support**]. Junk food availability at school prevents children from getting the nutrition they need for critical physical and mental development [**This is more Support**]. A recent study released by the USDA showed that recommended nutritional levels of children in schools with junk food in vending machines were almost [**The word "almost" is a Qualifier, tempering the statistic**] 30% lower than those in schools without [**This entire sentence is additional Support**]. Surveys conducted at numerous school districts in the Pacific Northwest showed that, when given the opportunity, most [**The word "most" is a Qualifier**] children would spend funds given them to purchase nutritional cafeteria food on junk food in vending machines [**This entire sentence is additional Support**].

Having healthier children is something this country values [**This sentence is the underlying assumption for the Claim; it is the Warrant**]. If junk food in public school vending machines is eliminated, we help improve the health of our children, which increases our prospects for sound, fit future citizens and reduces our nation's healthcare costs [**This sentence provides evidence for the Warrant; it is the Backing**].

While it can be said that junk food in small amounts is not harmful to children's diets [**The first part of this sentence is a Concession, recognizing a valid point of the opposition**], it remains a fact that our children are alarmingly overweight and school vending machines provide convenient opportunities for consumption of harmful foods without proper parental supervision of food choices **[The rest of the sentence refutes the opposition; it is a Rebuttal]**.

Vending machines have been identified as contributing significantly to revenue-strapped school districts and some feel that removing junk food from vending machines will reduce that revenue **[This sentence is another Concession to the opposing view]**. Eliminating junk food from vending machines and replacing it with healthy foods will still provide school districts revenue and children higher quality, healthier foods **[This sentence refutes the opposing view; it is a Rebuttal]**.

Here are the Toulmin elements of this piece specifically identified. As the outline shows, the support applies to the claim. The backing applies to the warrant. The concession and rebuttal are very closely connected. While in this example, that qualifier applies to the support, a qualifier could actually apply to all elements: claim, support, warrant, backing, concession, and rebuttal.

Claim: Junk food in public school vending machines should be banned.

Support: Junk food contributes to obesity, negatively impacts children's development, and uses funds that could be spent of healthy foods.

Warrant: Having healthy children is a good thing.

Backing: Healthier children will grow into better adults and will result in lower healthcare costs.

Concession/Rebuttal: Some junk food is not harmful but children need parental guidance; vending machines provide schools with revenue but can be stocked with healthy choices.

Qualifier: almost, most

Try copying and pasting this simple outline into a blank document and changing the topic. You might use a topic like banning cell phone use in restaurants or requiring all cities to use cameras to identify and ticket drivers who violate stoplight rules. Start out with your claim and then provide support for it. Try to find the underlying assumption that you are making (the warrant) for your claim (what is valuable about the end results of banning cell phone use in restaurants or ticketing drivers who run red lights?). Identify the kinds of information that back up that underlying assumption. Think about what the opposing viewpoints would look like. What would those who want to maintain the right to use cell phones in restaurants say? What kinds of responses would come from drivers who oppose stoplight enforcement through cameras? As you identify possible opposition, list concessions you might make to them. What options could be made for those who must have cell phones available at all times? What steps could be taken to relieve concerns about cameras invading drivers' privacy? Then try setting forth rebuttals you might make to their opposition, in light of the concessions you have made.

This brief examination of the Toulmin method of argument is designed to get you thinking about how to assess the validity of an argument and its underlying assumptions, how to challenge your opponent and how to concede when it is appropriate. If you would like to explore the Toulmin method further (and it is recommended that you do so), you can visit these helpful websites:

"The Toulmin Model of Argumentation" - Presented by San Diego State University

"Toulmin's Analysis" - Presented by LeTourneau University

"Writing Guide - The Toulmin Method" - Presented by Colorado State University

APPLYING THE TOULMIN METHOD TO OPPOSING ARGUMENTS

The Toulmin method is very useful when looking at opposing arguments. You can quickly determine strong and weak points of an opponent's case by looking at the claim, support, warrant, backing, and qualifiers. You can then determine what concessions and rebuttals might be most effective in your argument.

Try your hand at assessing an opposing argument by finding one that takes a stance that you would typically oppose. Read the piece carefully, using the critical reading skills identified in lesson three. As you look at the argument's claim, decide if it meets the standards set forth in lesson three. Is the argument's use of logos, ethos and/or pathos strong and effective? Does the opponent avoid logical fallacies? Are appeals appropriate and fair?

Next move your focus to the support or evidence that the opponent has provided to prove or validate the claim or claims. Is the supporting evidence sufficient, appropriate, and valid? Do you find yourself skeptical about data sources, relevance, and reliability?

The opponent's use of qualifiers should be examined. Is the argument filled with statements and terms that imply absolutes? Are qualifiers used in such a way that they enhance credibility? Or are qualifiers used so abundantly that the argument seems noncommittal?

The next step is examining the opponent's warrants. What assumption provides the foundation for the opponent's claim? Is each warrant one that is generally accepted by readers like you? Is it one that needs more evidence (backing)? What kind of additional support would be needed for you to agree with the warrant?

Then turn your attention on possible concessions. Are there points where the opposing view is quite strong, where you could comfortably admit that the opponent is on target? Identify why this point earns your support. Is it the result of additional data? Is the evidence from sources you trust? Is the point that you might concede something that is

widely accepted by readers like you?

Finally, look at possible rebuttals. Does the argument provide you good opportunities

to refute part or all of the claim? Does the evidence seem weak, irrelevant, outdated or

inadequate? What are the areas of vulnerability? How might you address those? What kinds

of evidence would you have to gather to build a strong rebuttal? Remember that a rebuttal is

in itself an argument. You will want to take the same careful steps preparing a rebuttal that

you do in building an entire argument.

As you conduct this review, it is helpful to keep the list of Toulmin terms in front of you.

Claim

Support

Qualifier

Warrant

Backing

Concession/Rebuttal

For additional practice, try applying the Toulmin method to the arguments you have read in

this lesson. For example, does Congresswoman Chisholm's claim that the Equal Rights

Amendment must be passed to prevent the "enshrinement" of prejudice in law stand up to

your scrutiny? Does she provide sufficient support (evidence) to convince you? Does she set

forth her argument with absolutes or does she use qualifiers so much that she weakens her

argument? What underlying assumption is at work in her argument? Do you see

opportunities for someone with an opposing view to make concessions? Do you find spots

where rebuttals would be effective?

Then try turning your attention to Carrie Chapman Catt's Congressional address. Is her claim about the inevitability and rightness of women's suffrage one you can accept? Does she provide sufficient evidence? Do you find Catt's "in your face" remarks to the members of Congress to be in need of qualifiers, to be toned down a bit? Or are they effective in the context of the entire argument? What underlying assumption (warrant) is at work here? Is Catt's warrant similar to that of Chisholm? If you were Catt's opponent, where might you make concessions to her? Where do you see good opportunities to refute her points?

Try applying the Toulmin method to both President Ford's address about pardoning Richard Nixon and Robert Kennedy's remarks about the assassination of Martin Luther King. Both pieces had similar goals, in that they were aimed at averting potential discord and protest following specific events. Both pieces had audiences full of daunting opponents. Both were given in an atmosphere of emotional intensity. Pay special attention to the warrants in each argument. What is the underlying assumption behind President Ford's claim? What is the warrant holding up Kennedy's argument? What value(s) is he hoping that Americans share? Are there areas where rebuttals seems viable to you?

Using the Toulmin method to assess opponents is an effective way to build a strong set of concessions and rebuttals and to anticipate the potential weak spots in your own argument.

CHOOSING A TOPIC FOR THE TOULMIN ESSAY

You have now had some experience working with the Toulmin method. In the next lesson, you will be writing your Toulmin essay. You should start getting ready for that essay by selecting your topic and starting your research.

How do you go about finding a topic to argue in the Toulmin method? Look carefully at the specific instructions for the assignment. Considering these limits, think about topics that are interesting to you. Is there an issue that you feel strongly about? Is there a topic that stirs your curiosity? Have you been puzzled by an issue in your locale? Have community members been upset by an issue? Have you wanted to immerse yourself in a topic, but haven't had time to do so? Examine agenda items of organizations you like or belong to. Do they have particular causes that are important to them? News media thrive on controversy. Are there events, issues or persons that have received media coverage, resulting in strong views on both sides? Draft a list of potential topics based on your answers to these questions.

Choose a number of topics that might work well and begin your research at the APUS Library. One good way to do some initial exploring is to use the APUS Library's Summon search engine, found in the center of the page when you get to the Library. Type in a word or phrase that represents your topic in the Search box. You do not have to have quote marks around the word. You will see a diagram on the left of your word/phrase, as well as other terms that may help you search. Clicking on those other terms will lead you to more possible topics for your argument.

There are other resources to help you with your research for your Toulmin argument. The APUS Library is one great place to start your quest.

CONCLUSION

This completes lesson four. Learning to analyze and respond appropriately to your opponents—learning to "negotiate opposition"—serves you well, as you can then utilize this knowledge and skill set to make your own arguments sounder and more convincing. Your exposure to the Toulmin method of argument gives you a new tool to apply to arguments, including those of your opponents. You can use the Toulmin checklist to test claims, evaluate evidence, and assess underlying assumptions, as well as test and build both concessions and rebuttals. This lesson sets the stage for your creation of a solid argument based on the Toulmin model. It also gives you new tools to respond to the many arguments you encounter every day.

QUESTIONS TO CONSIDER

1. What are some ways to enhance your credibility with an opponent?

2. What are effective ways to negotiate opposition?

3. A good summary of an opposing view should have what features?

4. What are the elements of the Toulmin argument?

5. How can the Toulmin method help in assessing an argument?

6. Where might you find good ideas for a Toulmin argument essay?

Works Cited

Ford, Gerald R. "Address to the Nation Pardoning Richard M. Nixon." *American Rhetoric.*

n.d. Web. Jan. 6, 2012.

Kennedy, Robert. F. "Remarks on the Assassination of Martin Luther King, Jr." *American*

Rhetoric. n.d. Web. Jan. 6, 2012.

St. Hill Chisholm, Shirley Anita. "For The Equal Rights Amendment." *American Rhetoric.* n.d.

Web. Jan. 6, 2012.

"Toulmin's Analysis." *LeTourneau University.* n.d. Web. 2012.

"The Toulmin Method of Argumentation." *ROHAN Academic Computing – San Diego*

State University. n.d. Web. 2012.

Wickins-Drazilova, Dita. "Zoo Animal Welfare." *Journal of Agricultural and Environmental*

Ethics 19.1 (2006): 27-36. *ABI/INFORM Global; ProQuest Religion; ProQuest*

Research Library. Web. 18 Jan. 2012.

"Writing Guide – The Toulmin Method." *Colorado State University.* 2003. Web. 2012.

READING SELECTIONS

Shirley Anita St. Hill Chisholm – "For the Equal Rights Amendment" - August 10, 1970

Mr. Speaker, House Joint Resolution 264, before us today, which provides for equality under the law for both men and women, represents one of the most clear-cut opportunities we are likely to have to declare our faith in the principles that shaped our Constitution. It provides a legal basis for attack on the most subtle, most pervasive, and most institutionalized form of prejudice that exists. Discrimination against women, solely on the basis of their sex, is so widespread that is seems to many persons normal, natural and right.

Legal expression of prejudice on the grounds of religious or political belief has become a minor problem in our society. Prejudice on the basis of race is, at least, under systematic attack. Their [sic] is reason for optimism that it will start to die with the present, older generation. It is time we act to assure full equality of opportunity to those citizens who, although in a majority, suffer the restrictions that are commonly imposed on minorities, to women.

The argument that this amendment will not solve the problem of sex discrimination is not relevant. If the argument were used against a civil rights bill, as it has been used in the past, the prejudice that lies behind it would be embarrassing. Of course laws will not eliminate prejudice from the hearts of human beings. But that is no reason to allow prejudice to continue to be enshrined in our laws -- to perpetuate injustice through inaction.

The amendment is necessary to clarify countless ambiguities and inconsistencies in our legal system. For instance, the Constitution guarantees due process of law, in the 5th and 14th amendments. But the applicability of due process of sex distinctions is not clear. Women are excluded from some State colleges and universities. In some States, restrictions are placed on a married woman who engages in an independent business. Women may not be chosen for some juries. Women even receive heavier criminal penalties than men who commit the same crime. What would the legal effects of the equal rights amendment really be? The equal rights amendment would govern only the relationship between the State and its citizens -- not relationships between private citizens. The amendment would be largely self-executing, that is, and Federal or State laws in conflict would be ineffective one year after date of ratification without further action by the Congress or State legislatures.

Opponents of the amendment claim its ratification would throw the law into a state of confusion and would result in much litigation to establish its meaning. This objection overlooks the influence of legislative history in determining intent and the recent activities of many groups preparing for legislative changes in this direction.

State labor laws applying only to women, such as those limiting hours of work and weights to be lifted would become inoperative unless the legislature amended them to apply to men. As of early 1970 most States would have some laws that would be affected. However, changes are being made so rapidly as a result of title VII of the Civil Rights Act of 1964, it is likely that by the time the equal rights amendment would become effective; no confliction [sic] State laws would remain.

In any event, there has for years been great controversy as to the usefulness to women of these State labor laws. There has never been any doubt that they worked a hardship on women who need or want to work overtime and on women who need or want better paying jobs, and there has been no persuasive evidence as to how many women benefit from the archaic policy of the laws. After the Delaware hours law was repealed in 1966, there were no complaints from women to any of the State agencies that might have been approached.

Jury service laws not making women equally liable for jury service would have been revised. The selective service law would have to include women, but women would not be required to serve in the Armed Forces where they are not fitted any more than men are required to serve. Military service, while a great responsibility, is not without benefits, particularly for young men with limited education or training.

Since October 1966, 246,000 young men who did not meet the normal mental or physical requirements have been given opportunities for training and correcting physical problems. This opportunity is not open to their sisters. Only girls who have completed high school and meet high standards on the educational test can volunteer. Ratification of the amendment would not permit application of higher standards to women.

Survivorship benefits would be available to husbands of female workers on the same basis as to wives of male workers. The Social Security Act and the civil service and military service retirement acts are in conflict. Public schools and universities could not be limited to one sex and could not apply different admission standards to men and women. Laws requiring longer prison sentences for women than men would be invalid, and equal opportunities for rehabilitation and vocational training would have to be provided in public correctional institutions. Different ages of majority based on sex would have to be harmonized. Federal, State, and other governmental bodies would be obligated to follow nondiscriminatory practices in all aspects of employment, including public school teachers and State university and college faculties.

What would be the economic effects of the equal rights amendment? Direct economic effects would be minor. If any labor laws applying only to women still remained, their amendment or repeal would provide opportunity for women in better-paying jobs in manufacturing. More opportunities in public vocational and graduate schools for women would also tend to open up opportunities in better jobs for women.

Indirect effects could be much greater. The focusing of public attention on the gross legal, economic, and social discrimination against women by hearings and debates in the Federal and State legislatures would result in changes in attitude of parents, educators, and employers that would bring about substantial economic changes in the long run.

Sex prejudice cuts both ways. Men are oppressed by the requirements of the Selective Service Act, by enforced legal guardianship of minors, and by alimony laws. Each sex, I believe, should be liable when necessary to serve and defend this country. Each has a responsibility for the support of children.

There are objections raised to wiping out laws protecting women workers. No one would condone exploitation. But what does sex have to do with it. [sic] Working conditions and hours that are harmful to women are harmful to men; wages that are unfair for women are unfair for men. Laws setting employment limitations on the basis of sex are irrational, and the proof of this is their inconsistency from State to State. The physical characteristics of men and women are not fixed, but cover two wide spans that have a great deal of overlap. It is obvious, I think, that a robust woman could be more fit for physical labor than a weak man. The choice of occupation would be determined by individual capabilities, and the rewards for equal works should be equal.

This is what it comes down to: artificial distinctions between persons must be wiped out of the law. Legal discrimination between the sexes is, in almost every instance, founded on outmoded views of society and the pre-scientific beliefs about psychology and physiology. It is time to sweep away these relics of the past and set further generations free of them.

Federal agencies and institutions responsible for the enforcement of equal opportunity laws need the authority of a Constitutional amendment. The 1964 Civil Rights Act and the 1963 Equal Pay Act are not enough; they are limited in their coverage – for instance, one excludes teachers, and the other leaves out administrative and professional women. The Equal Employment Opportunity Commission has not proven to be an adequate device, with its power limited to investigation, conciliation, and recommendation to the Justice Department. In its cases involving sexual discrimination, it has failed in more than one-half. The Justice Department has been even less effective. It has intervened in only one case involving discrimination on the basis of sex, and this was on a procedural point. In a second case, in which both sexual and racial discrimination were alleged, the racial bias charge was given far greater weight.

Evidence of discrimination on the basis of sex should hardly have to be cited here. It is in the Labor Department's employment and salary figures for anyone who is still in doubt. Its elimination will involve so many changes in our State and Federal laws that, without the authority and impetus of this proposed amendment, it will perhaps take another 194 years. We cannot be parties to continuing a delay. The time is clearly now to put this House on record for the fullest expression of that equality of opportunity which our founding fathers professed. They professed it, but they did not assure it to their daughters, as they tried to do for their sons.

The Constitution they wrote was designed to protect the rights of white, male citizens. As there were no black Founding Fathers, there were no founding mothers – a great pity, on both counts. It is not too late to complete the work they left undone. Today, here, we should start to do so.

In closing I would like to make one point. Social and psychological effects will be initially more important than legal or economic results. As Leo Kanowitz has pointed out:

Rules of law that treat of [sic] the sexes per see [sic] inevitably produce far-reaching effects upon social, psychological and economic aspects of male-female relations beyond the limited confines of legislative chambers and courtrooms. As long as organized legal systems, at once the most respected and most feared of social institutions, continue to differentiate sharply, in treatment or in words, between men and women on the basis of irrelevant and artificially created distinctions, the likelihood of men and women coming to regard one another primarily as fellow human beings and only secondarily as representatives of another sex will continue to be remote. When men and women are prevented from recognizing one another's essential humanity by sexual prejudices, nourished by legal as well as social institutions, society as a whole remains less than it could otherwise become.

Gerald R. Ford –"Address to the Nation Pardoning Richard M. Nixon" – September 8, 1974

Ladies and gentlemen: I have come to a decision which I felt I should tell you and all of my fellow American citizens, as soon as I was certain in my own mind and in my own conscience that it is the right thing to do. I have learned already in this office that the difficult decisions always come to this desk. I must admit that many of them do not look at all the same as the hypothetical questions that I have answered freely and perhaps too fast on previous occasions.

My customary policy is to try and get all the facts and to consider the opinions of my countrymen and to take counsel with my most valued friends. But these seldom agree, and in the end, the decision is mine. To procrastinate, to agonize, and to wait for a more favorable turn of events that may never come or more compelling external pressures that may as well be wrong as right, is itself a decision of sorts and a weak and potentially dangerous course for a President to follow.

I have promised to uphold the Constitution, to do what is right as God gives me to see the right, and to do the very best that I can for America. I have asked your help and your prayers, not only when I became President but many times since. The Constitution is the supreme law of our land, and it governs our actions as citizens. Only the laws of God, which govern our consciences, are superior to it.

As we are a nation under God, so I am sworn to uphold our laws with the help of God. And I have sought such guidance and searched my own conscience with special diligence to determine the right thing for me to do with respect to my predecessor in this place, Richard Nixon, and his loyal wife and family. Theirs is an American tragedy in which we all -- all have played a part. It could go on and on and on, or someone must write the end to it. I have concluded that only I can do that, and if I can, I must.

There are no historic or legal precedents to which I can turn in this matter, none that precisely fit the circumstances of a private citizen who has resigned the Presidency of the United States. But it is common knowledge that serious allegations and accusations hang like a sword over our former President's head, threatening his health as he tries to reshape his life, a great part of which was spent in the service of this country and by the mandate of its people.

After years of bitter controversy and divisive national debate, I have been advised, and I am compelled to conclude that many months and perhaps more years will have to pass before Richard Nixon could obtain a fair trial by jury in any jurisdiction of the United States under governing decisions of the Supreme Court. I deeply believe in equal justice for all Americans, whatever their station or former station. The law, whether human or divine, is no respecter of persons; but the law is a respecter of reality.

The facts, as I see them, are that a former President of the United States, instead of enjoying equal treatment with any other citizen accused of violating the law, would be cruelly and excessively penalized either in preserving the presumption of his innocence or in obtaining a speedy determination of his guilt in order to repay a legal debt to society. During this long period of delay and potential litigation, ugly passions would again be aroused. And our people would again be polarized in their opinions. And the credibility of our free institutions of government would again be challenged at home and abroad. In the end, the courts might well hold that Richard Nixon had been denied due process, and the verdict of history would even more be inconclusive with respect to those charges arising out of the period of his Presidency, of which I am presently aware.

But it is not the ultimate fate of Richard Nixon that most concerns me, though surely it deeply troubles every decent and every compassionate person. My concern is the immediate future of this great country. In this, I dare not depend upon my personal sympathy as a long-time friend of the former President, nor my professional judgment as a lawyer, and I do not.

As President, my primary concern must always be the greatest good of all the people of the United States whose servant I am. As a man, my first consideration is to be true to my own convictions and my own conscience. My conscience tells me clearly and certainly that I cannot prolong the bad dreams that continue to reopen a chapter that is closed. My conscience tells me that only I, as President, have the constitutional power to firmly shut and seal this book. My conscience tells me it is my duty, not merely to proclaim domestic tranquility but to use every means that I have to insure it.

I do believe that the buck stops here, that I cannot rely upon public opinion polls to tell me what is right.

I do believe that right makes might and that if I am wrong, 10 angels swearing I was right would make no difference.

I do believe, with all my heart and mind and spirit, that I, not as President but as a humble servant of God, will receive justice without mercy if I fail to show mercy.

Finally, I feel that Richard Nixon and his loved ones have suffered enough and will continue to suffer, no matter what I do, no matter what we, as a great and good nation, can do together to make his goal of peace come true.

Now, therefore, I, Gerald R. Ford, President of the United States, pursuant to the pardon power conferred upon me by Article II, Section 2, of the Constitution, have granted and by these presents do grant a full, free, and absolute pardon unto Richard Nixon for all offenses against the United States which he, Richard Nixon, has committed or may have committed or taken part in during the period from July 20, 1969 through August 9, 1974.

In witness whereof, I have hereunto set my hand this eighth day of September, in the year of our Lord nineteen hundred and seventy-four, and of the Independence of the United States of America the one hundred and ninety-ninth.

Robert F. Kennedy –"Remarks on the Assassination of Martin Luther King, Jr." – April 4, 1968

Ladies and Gentlemen,

I'm only going to talk to you just for a minute or so this evening, because I have some -- some very sad news for all of you -- Could you lower those signs, please? -- I have some very sad news for all of you, and, I think, sad news for all of our fellow citizens, and people who love peace all over the world; and that is that Martin Luther King was shot and was killed tonight in Memphis, Tennessee.

Martin Luther King dedicated his life to love and to justice between fellow human beings. He died in the cause of that effort. In this difficult day, in this difficult time for the United States, it's perhaps well to ask what kind of a nation we are and what direction we want to move in. For those of you who are black -- considering the evidence evidently is that there were white people who were responsible -- you can be filled with bitterness, and with hatred, and a desire for revenge.

We can move in that direction as a country, in greater polarization -- black people amongst blacks, and white amongst whites, filled with hatred toward one another. Or we can make an effort, as Martin Luther King did, to understand, and to comprehend, and replace that violence, that stain of bloodshed that has spread across our land, with an effort to understand, compassion, and love.

For those of you who are black and are tempted to fill with -- be filled with hatred and mistrust of the injustice of such an act, against all white people, I would only say that I can also feel in my own heart the same kind of feeling. I had a member of my family killed, but he was killed by a white man.

But we have to make an effort in the United States. We have to make an effort to understand, to get beyond, or go beyond these rather difficult times.

My favorite poem, my -- my favorite poet was Aeschylus. And he once wrote:

Even in our sleep, pain which cannot forget
falls drop by drop upon the heart,
until, in our own despair,
against our will,
comes wisdom
through the awful grace of God.

What we need in the United States is not division; what we need in the United States is not hatred; what we need in the United States is not violence and lawlessness, but is love, and wisdom, and compassion toward one another, and a feeling of justice toward those who still suffer within our country, whether they be white or whether they be black.

So I ask you tonight to return home, to say a prayer for the family of Martin Luther King -- yeah, it's true -- but more importantly to say a prayer for our own country, which all of us love -- a prayer for understanding and that compassion of which I spoke.

We can do well in this country. We will have difficult times. We've had difficult times in the past, but we -- and we will have difficult times in the future. It is not the end of violence; it is not the end of lawlessness; and it's not the end of disorder.

But the vast majority of white people and the vast majority of black people in this country want to live together, want to improve the quality of our life, and want justice for all human beings that abide in our land.

And let's dedicate ourselves to what the Greeks wrote so many years ago: to tame the savageness of man and make gentle the life of this world. Let us dedicate ourselves to that, and say a prayer for our country and for our people.

Thank you very much.

Carrie Chapman Catt –"Address to the Congress on Women's Suffrage" – November 1917

Woman suffrage is inevitable. Suffragists knew it before November 4, 1917; opponents afterward. Three distinct causes made it inevitable.

First, the history of our country. Ours is a nation born of revolution, of rebellion against a system of government so securely entrenched in the customs and traditions of human society that in 1776 it seemed impregnable. From the beginning of things, nations had been ruled by kings and for kings, while the people served and paid the cost. The American Revolutionists boldly proclaimed the heresies: "Taxation without representation is tyranny." "Governments derive their just powers from the consent of the governed." The colonists won, and the nation which was established as a result of their victory has held unfailingly that these two fundamental principles of democratic government are not only the spiritual source of our national existence but have been our chief historic pride and at all times the sheet anchor of our liberties.

Eighty years after the Revolution, Abraham Lincoln welded those two maxims into a new one: "Ours is a government of the people, by the people, and for the people." Fifty years more passed and the president of the United States, Woodrow Wilson, in a mighty crisis of the nation, proclaimed to the world: "We are fighting for the things which we have always carried nearest to our hearts: for democracy, for the right of those who submit to authority to have a voice in their own government."

All the way between these immortal aphorisms political leaders have declared unabated faith in their truth. Not one American has arisen to question their logic in the 141 years of our national existence. However stupidly our country may have evaded the logical application at times, it has never swerved from its devotion to the theory of democracy as expressed by those two axioms...

With such a history behind it, how can our nation escape the logic it has never failed to follow, when its last un-enfranchised class calls for the vote? Behold our Uncle Sam floating the banner with one hand, "Taxation without representation is tyranny," and with the other seizing the billions of dollars paid in taxes by women to whom he refuses "representation." Behold him again, welcoming the boys of twenty-one and the newly made immigrant citizen to "a voice in their own government" while he denies that fundamental right of democracy to thousands of women public school teachers from whom many of these men learn all they know of citizenship and patriotism, to women college presidents, to women who preach in our pulpits, interpret law in our courts, preside over our hospitals, write books and magazines, and serve in every uplifting moral and social enterprise. Is there a single man who can justify such inequality of treatment, such outrageous discrimination? Not one...

Second, the suffrage for women already established in the United States makes women suffrage for the nation inevitable. When Elihu Root, as president of the American Society of International Law, at the eleventh annual meeting in Washington, April 26, 1917, said, "The world cannot be half democratic and half autocratic. It must be all democratic or all Prussian. There can be no compromise," he voiced a general truth. Precisely the same intuition has already taught the blindest and most hostile foe of woman suffrage that our nation cannot long continue a condition under which government in half its territory rests upon the consent of half of the people and in the other half upon the consent of all the people; a condition which grants representation to the taxed in half of its territory and denies it in the other half; a condition which permits women in some states to share in the election of the president, senators, and representatives and denies them that privilege in others. It is too obvious to require demonstration that woman suffrage, now covering half our territory, will eventually be ordained in all the nation. No one will deny it. The only question left is when and how will it be completely established.

Third, the leadership of the United States in world democracy compels the enfranchisement of its own women. The maxims of the Declaration were once called "fundamental principles of government." They are now called "American principles" or even "Americanisms." They have become the slogans of every movement toward political liberty the world around, of every effort to widen the suffrage for men or women in any land. Not a people, race, or class striving for freedom is there anywhere in the world that has not made our axioms the chief weapon of the struggle. More, all men and women the world around, with farsighted vision into the verities of things, know that the world tragedy of our day is not now being waged over the assassination of an archduke, nor commercial competition, nor national ambitions, nor the freedom of the seas. It is a death grapple between the forces which deny and those which uphold the truths of the Declaration of Independence...

Do you realize that in no other country in the world with democratic tendencies is suffrage so completely denied as in a considerable number of our own states? There are thirteen black states where no suffrage for women exists, and fourteen others where suffrage for women is more limited than in many foreign countries.

Do you realize that when you ask women to take their cause to state referendum you compel them to do this: that you drive women of education, refinement, achievement, to beg men who cannot read for their political freedom?

Do you realize that such anomalies as a college president asking her janitor to give her a vote are overstraining the patience and driving women to desperation?

Do you realize that women in increasing numbers indignantly resent the long delay in their enfranchisement?

Your party platforms have pledged women suffrage. Then why not be honest, frank friends of our cause, adopt it in reality as your own, make it a party program, and "fight with us"? As a party measure -- a measure of all parties -- why not put the amendment through Congress and the legislatures? We shall all be better friends, we shall have a happier nation, we women will be free to support loyally the party of our choice, and we shall be far prouder of our history.

"There is one thing mightier than kings and armies" -- aye, than Congresses and political parties – "the power of an idea when its time has come to move." The time for woman suffrage has come. The woman's hour has struck. If parties prefer to postpone action longer and thus do battle with this idea, they challenge the inevitable. The idea will not perish; the party which opposes it may. Every delay, every trick, every political dishonesty from now on will antagonize the women of the land more and more, and when the party or parties which have so delayed woman suffrage finally let it come, their sincerity will be doubted and their appeal to the new voters will be met with suspicion. This is the psychology of the situation. Can you afford the risk? Think it over.

We know you will meet opposition. There are a few "women haters" left, a few "old males of the tribe," as Vance Thompson calls them, whose duty they believe it to be to keep women in the places they have carefully picked out for them. Treitschke, made world famous by war literature, said some years ago, "Germany, which knows all about Germany and France, knows far better what is good for Alsace-Lorraine than that miserable people can possibly know." A few American Treitschkes we have who know better than women what is good for them. There are women, too, with "slave souls" and "clinging vines" for backbones. There are female dolls and male dandies. But the world does not wait for such as these, nor does liberty pause to heed the plaint of men and women with a grouch. She does not wait for those who have a special interest to serve, nor a selfish reason for depriving other people of freedom. Holding her torch aloft, liberty is pointing the way onward and upward and saying to America, "Come."

To you and the supporters of our cause in Senate and House, and the number is large, the suffragists of the nation express their grateful thanks. This address is not meant for you. We are more truly appreciative of all you have done than any words can express. We ask you to make a last, hard fight for the amendment during the present session. Since last we asked a vote on this amendment, your position has been fortified by the addition to suffrage territory of Great Britain, Canada, and New York.

Some of you have been too indifferent to give more than casual attention to this question. It is worthy of your immediate consideration. A question big enough to engage the attention of our allies in wartime is too big a question for you to neglect.

Some of you have grown old in party service. Are you willing that those who take your places by and by shall blame you for having failed to keep pace with the world and thus having lost for them a party advantage? Is there any real gain for you, for your party, for your nation by delay? Do you want to drive the progressive men and women out of your party?

Some of you hold to the doctrine of states' rights as applying to woman suffrage. Adherence to that theory will keep the United States far behind all other democratic nations upon this question. A theory which prevents a nation from keeping up with the trend of world progress cannot be justified.

Gentlemen, we hereby petition you, our only designated representatives, to redress our grievances by the immediate passage of the Federal Suffrage Amendment and to use your influence to secure its ratification in your own state, in order that the women of our nation may be endowed with political freedom before the next presidential election, and that our nation may resume its world leadership in democracy.

Woman suffrage is coming -- you know it. Will you, Honorable Senators and Members of the House of Representatives, help or hinder it?

Chapter 5: Using the Toulmin Method Continued, Creating Argumentative Claims, Using Reliable Sources

Introduction

Lesson five continues to explore the Toulmin argument method, providing more specific assistance as you build your Toulmin essay. You will spend time moving your argument from topic choice to final draft. As part of your work on the Toulmin method, you will look at types of claims typically found in these arguments (fact, problem-based, definition, evaluation, and cause), and you will also spend more time examining warrants, the assumptions underlying the claims. You will also work on determining reliability of sources and citing and documenting sources used in your paper. The topics covered in this and previous lessons will prepare you for demonstrating that you can critically evaluate a piece of writing.

Organization

Have you ever heard students say that they write best by just sitting down and starting to write? Have you heard folks say that they don't do well when they have to plan papers, when they have to have an organizational scheme in mind when they begin? Are you a writer who feels your best work is spontaneous rather than carefully organized? If that is the case, can you identify why you feel this way? Have you struggled with organizing your writing in the past?

The spontaneous approach may work well for some kinds of writing, but argument is not typically one of them. A good argument requires painstaking care and planning. To be effective, a good argument will typically involve much work before the first sentence is ever drafted.

It's safe to say that argument essays are among the most formal you will write. Argument is an art. Argument is also a science. The rigors of science will apply to much of what is covered in this lesson, beginning with the core of an argument, the claim.

TYPES OF CLAIMS

You learned in the last lesson that a claim sets forth the writer's opinion on the topic, the stance the writer is taking, the point the writer is going to make. A claim may be called a proposition or a thesis, the single statement that connects all elements of the argument. A claim is the statement that the writer is asking the reader to accept as true. Claims can take many forms depending on what stance the writer is taking. Five kinds of claims will be covered in this lesson:

1. Claim of Fact

2. Problem-based Claim (sometimes called a Claim of Policy)

3. Claim of Definition

4. Claim of Evaluation

5. Claim of Cause

CLAIM OF FACT

A claim of fact is a statement that something exists, did exist or will exist. This kind of claim is an assertion that something is true or untrue. Facts are sometimes defined as bits of information or conditions that can be observed and are distinguished from opinions, which are regarded as depending solely on conviction or belief. An argument that is based on a claim of fact often uses the verb "is," since it asserts that something is true or untrue: *this is the way it is*. For example, this statement would be a claim of fact: *Stoplight violations* *in Plainsville have increased by 26% in the last twelve months.* This claim says "This is how is it in Plainsville regarding drivers running red and yellow lights." The writer's job on this claim is to provide examples, statistics, expert testimony and other evidence to convince the reader that this is the current situation in the community. Primary evidence for such a claim may include statistics about violations, to convince the reader that this snapshot is an accurate one.

PROBLEM-BASED CLAIM

Where a claim of fact asserts *this is the way it is,* a **problem-based claim** asserts *this is the way it ought to be.* A problem-based claim suggests what should be done to solve a problem, often declaring that one course of action is superior to another. Verbs such as ought, should or must are typical in these claims. This statement is a problem-based (or policy) claim: *Camera enforcement should be implemented at all Plainsville intersections with stoplights.*

The reader needs to be convinced, first, that there is a problem and, second, that this is the best solution. So the principles guiding the claim of fact apply here as well, in that the problem has to be presented in a convincing way. The reader needs to feel that action is needed. A problem-based claim also needs to include an explanation of the solution, so the reader knows precisely what the solution will look like. In addition, this kind of claim needs to address values to some degree, in that the reader needs to know why the solution being presented is preferred over other options. In the example of camera enforcement at stoplights, the writer would need to convince the reader that there is a problem with stoplight violations in Plainsville, explain to the reader how camera surveillance works to enforce compliance with stoplight requirements, and persuade the reader that camera enforcement will reduce stoplight violations.

Evidence for this claim would include statistics on stoplight violations and resultant accidents, with emphasis on those involving injury and death. Evidence might also include expert testimony from officials in other cities where the approach has been effective in reducing violations and accidents.

CLAIM OF DEFINITION

A claim of definition helps the reader understand in which category a person, thing, act, or event belongs or does not belong. Why does putting items in categories matter? Categorization helps us sort through the vast bank of data we receive each day; it helps us make sense of the world. In arguments, categories help us understand which option might be best for our support. This statement is a claim of definition: *Camera surveillance at stoplights does not constitute a "violation of privacy rights" of drivers.* In this example, the category of "violation of privacy rights" is being explored and the writer will work to prove that camera surveillance does not fit in that category.

Evidence for a claim of definition may include examples to show how the thing being contested either fits or does not fit in the category. It may also include expert testimony about the category itself. You may have seen arguments about gun control in which a primary focus is defining the constitutional guarantee of the right to bear arms. In the example used in this lesson, the argument on camera surveillance at stoplights may include evidence of court cases in which judges and juries have determined that this kind of enforcement does not violate drivers' rights to privacy.

CLAIM OF EVALUATION

A claim of evaluation asserts that something is good or bad. It answers the question "What is the worth or value of this thing?" It sets forth a specific set of criteria related to ethics or goodness and shows the reader how the thing being argued meets these criteria. A claim of evaluation may often involve a comparison of the item being promoted in the argument with other options. The writer's task here is to demonstrate how the proposed option meets the criteria of "goodness," how it surpasses other options in addressing underlying concerns. This statement is a claim of evaluation: *Camera surveillance is the most cost-effective way to enforce stoplight violations in Plainsville.*

Evidence in this case may include expert testimony from officials in other communities where a variety of options have been tried. It may also include statistics on the costs and results of other enforcement approaches, including the use of police officers posted at intersections. Results of trials for offenders, possibly those involving fatal accidents, could be included. The writer could look at the costs of trials resulting in convictions, comparing the costs of those involving camera surveillance to the costs of those without.

CLAIM OF CAUSE

A claim of cause looks at the causes or effects (consequences) of something. It answers the question "What are the causes of this event/thing?" or "What are the consequences of this event/thing?" The claim of cause looks beyond sequential relationships (first this happens, then that happens) to causal relationships (this happened, which then resulted in that happening). In this kind of claim the writer typically uses a chronological process to set forth links in a chain of events or to propose possible consequences of an action. This is a claim of cause: *Drivers' failure to comply with stoplight requirements resulted in 12 more fatal accidents in Plainsville in 2011 than in the previous year.*

Evidence in a claim of cause could take the forms listed above, including facts, statistics, and expert testimony, as well as logos, pathos, and ethos. For the stoplight example, accident and fatality statistics could be used, as well as testimony from experts in the fields of public safety and insurance.

The writer should be especially careful, in constructing this kind of claim, to avoid the logical fallacy of *post hoc, ergo propter hoc*, that is, after that, therefore because of that. This fallacy (explained in lesson three) substitutes a causal relationship where in fact only a sequential relationship exists.

PRACTICE IDENTIFYING TYPES OF CLAIMS

Having reviewed these five types of claims, practice applying this information by returning to the arguments covered in lesson four. These specific questions can guide you.

1. What type of claim provides the major focus of Shirley Chisholm's Congressional address about the Equal Rights Amendment? Is it a claim of fact, problem-based claim, or claim of definition, evaluation or cause? Why do you feel that way? Does her evidence adequately support that kind of claim?

2. Examine the speech made by Carrie Chapman Catt concerning women's suffrage. She begins her argument with three paragraphs that each start with a specific transitional word (first, second, third). As you read those three paragraphs, determine what kind of claim she is presenting. Is it a claim of fact, problem-based claim, or claim of definition, evaluation or cause? Why do you feel that way? Does her evidence adequately support that kind of claim?

3. In the essay "Zoo Animal Welfare," by Dr. Dita Wickins-Drazilova, examine how the author explores the definition of "zoo." Pay special attention to the last part of her

argument. Does she provide criteria for the reader to use in defining the term? Does her definition of "zoo" match yours? Why do you feel that way?

Being able to distinguish among different kinds of claims is helpful to you, both as a reader and a writer. You can assess the quality of sources you may use; you can review opposing viewpoints to see opportunities for concession and rebuttal; and you can build an argument that is appropriate for your intent and support it with the kind of evidence that will effectively convince your reader.

SUPPORTING YOUR CLAIM

Once you have decided what kind of claim you are going to use, you need to begin compiling the support for it. You should review your research, notes and observations, to see what kinds of supporting evidence you can provide. Some writers ask how much evidence is required. Although no two arguments are the same, for an academic essay similar to your Toulmin argument, it is common to see at least three major "branches" of support. There is nothing magic about the number three, but this number allows you to provide a broad range of evidence. Should one kind of evidence be determined by the reader to be refutable, two more remain which can still sway a reader.

What forms should your support take? Support is composed of evidence that a writer uses to prove the claim. Support is usually a combination of facts and reasoning. It may include statistics, data, expert testimony, interviews, surveys, observations, and persuasive appeals of logos, ethos, and pathos, as described in lesson three.

You should examine evidence you will use for your support to make sure it is sufficient. Do you have enough data to be convincing? If examples are used, are there enough to see a meaningful trend? If a survey is used, are there enough respondents? Your evidence should be relevant to your topic and it should be accurate. How do you determine accuracy? That is a challenge, but one way is to use reliable sources, as explained in lesson two. Another is to check the sources listed in the bibliography of a source you are using. You can often double-check data you find in a source by tracking the origin of that information. Your evidence should be recent. The internet makes it easier to find evidence that is very current; however, as explained in lesson two, take the time to find the latest reliable research on your topic. It should also be representative, that is, typical of the items or group discussed in your argument.

Support can also take the form of persuasive appeals (logos, ethos, and pathos). Please see lesson three for a thorough discussion of these appeals.

Sources

As you compile the support for your claim, you should pay special attention to the sources you are using. The strength of your argument will depend, to a great extent, on the strength of these sources. You should be vigilant about choosing sources that will serve you well. Lesson two provided you some good suggestions for selecting academic sources. Here are additional ideas.

One of the first things to look at is the identity of the source. You should be wary of facts, statistics, or findings that are set forth without the origin of this information. Phrases such as "a recent study" or "scientists have found" serve as red flags, alerting you that the evidence may not be right for your essay. Sometimes the origin of the evidence will be provided in footnotes, a works cited entry, or a bibliography. If you cannot find where the evidence came from, be cautious about using it.

When you do find the source of the information, assess it carefully. Government, military, and academic sources are more likely to provide objective, balanced evidence than are commercial entities or industry associations since their funding (and thus existence) is not exclusively based on pleasing stockholders or corporate members. Information from special interest groups should be used with care, again because objectivity and balance may be questionable.

If the evidence you are looking at comes from a purported expert in the field, be sure to look at the person's credentials, including educational and employment background as well as professional organizations the he or she may associated with. If possible verify those credentials.

If your evidence comes from a website, be sure to investigate the site thoroughly. Typically a website whose URL ends with *gov, mil* or *edu* tends to be a more credible source than one that ends in *com* or *org* since the motivation of the last two may be primarily focused on profit or advocacy. A website without contact information, explanation of mission, and disclosure of authors as well as ties to organizations or businesses is suspect. Check the currency of posts on a website and, if you can, the accuracy of postings.

If your evidence comes from a publication, study it. Determine who publishes it (lobbying organizations, special interest groups, and faith-based entities may have specific agendas). In the case of journals, those that are peer-reviewed, that is, evaluated by experts in that field, or published by a university press offer information that is typically credible.

You may find that as you explore your topic you encounter certain studies, persons, or groups repeatedly. If one credible source refers to another, that is usually a good sign. Your time familiarizing yourself with your topic will be well spent, as it will help you identify sources that you can count on.

Taking time to choose your sources carefully is an essential part of building an effective argument. Don't take shortcuts on this step as the strength of your support depends on having solid evidence from good sources.

WARRANTS

You learned in the last lesson that a warrant is an underlying assumption or inference that the writer takes for granted. The warrant sets up an agreement between the writer and reader that the issue at hand is an important one, spelling out what the reader has to assume so the argument can work. Warrants are often based on cultural values or belief systems that the writer and reader share. They do not have to be specifically stated but can be implied. Recognizing warrants is a critical skill because, if a reader does not agree with the underlying assumption that the writer takes for granted, it is unlikely that the writer's claim will be accepted. If you do not know what warrants are underlying your claims, you may construct an argument that can be easily defeated.

Because warrants are so important, you will be spending additional time studying them in this lesson. When you think about warrants, it is helpful to think about how we use the word "warrant" in our conversations and writings. You have probably heard persons say "This warrants further attention" or "It didn't warrant more discussion." To warrant something is to justify it, to make it seem reasonable and important. So, in the Toulmin argument system, the warrant justifies the claim, makes it seem reasonable and important. The warrant links the claim with the support (evidence) and gives the reader reason to make that connection.

Warrants may be based on the types of persuasive appeals you studied in lesson three: logos (logic), ethos (authority), and pathos (emotions). They may also be based on shared values and beliefs. For example, the United States' Constitution and Bill of Rights are formalized statements of shared values and beliefs and many tenets of these documents serve as warrants for arguments. The right to bear arms and the right to free speech are two values that Americans share. Can you think of an argument you have read or heard that uses one of these two rights as an underlying assumption, a warrant?

Warrants may also be general principles or "rules" of specific disciplines. Biologists, for example, typically conduct, document, and present findings of research using very specific methods that are well established and accepted by other biologists. These govern how research is set up, carried out, and compiled. The shared values of biological research are formalized into written standards (conventions) that are accepted and shared. A claim made by a biological researcher will often be backed by these principles, which may typically not be expressed. For example, a key warrant for many biological claims may be that all creatures deserve protection from cruelty and harm. So research conducted on, say, pronghorn antelopes, should be done in ways that protect them from harm. It is unlikely than any argument about them from wildlife biologists would specifically state that, but the commitment to their protection is key. Research methods would be developed based on the premise of avoiding harm to the animals. This is a shared value, an accepted convention, an underlying assumption, a warrant.

BACKING

As indicated in lesson four, sometimes a warrant is not widely known or accepted and must be defended. In the case mentioned above, the warrant of protecting pronghorn antelope from harm may not need to be explicitly stated for audiences made of up of biologists. But for lay audiences, or possibly public officials, it may be necessary that this warrant be specifically stated and supported. As you learned earlier, a warrant's evidence is called "backing." Backing may take the same form as support for a claim (facts, statistics, logic, expert testimony and so on). A warrant's backing statements are also subject to the same evaluation as are other forms of evidence (reliable, current, sufficient, free of logical fallacies, etc.).

For an example of warrants and backing, look at the executive order issued by Governor Paul LePage of Maine: <u>"An Order Regarding the Use of Green Building Standards in State Buildings."</u> The executive order issued by Maine's governor requires that any new or "expanded" state building construction is to use "Green Building" standards as part of its design, construction, operation, and maintenance. You will see that the executive order is organized with a number of "whereas" statements, followed by "therefore" statements. Look at the list of "whereas" statements, summarized here. Governor LePage says that the following are important:

- Whereas Maine is dedicated to the goals of energy efficiency, environmental protection, and economic growth;

- Whereas the State should undertake initiatives that foster cost efficient and ecologically responsible buildings;

- Whereas reducing long-term operations and maintenance costs is essential to the economic health of the State;

- Whereas Green Building standards have the potential to reduce waste in building;

- Whereas the standards have requirements on the harvest of natural construction, some of which recognize equally several forest certifications systems used in Maine and North America;

- Whereas Maine is a national leader in the processing and availability of certified sustainable construction materials;

- Whereas recognizing these certifications will promote sustainable forestry in Maine and help protect and develop good jobs while maintaining the State's strong outdoor heritage.

As you look at this list, can you identify underlying assumptions, beliefs, and values that are shared by citizens and organizations in Maine? For example, how many shared values do you see represented in the last item? Notice how the sustainable forest industry, good jobs, and outdoor heritage are set forth in this item to gather support for the Governor's claim (that Green Building standards be applied to new construction and significant modification of state buildings). The Governor is relying on citizens' support, because he knows they want jobs, they want to protect the environment, and they want to preserve their state's outdoor heritage.

This executive order is not an argument essay. It is, however, an outline that clearly shows how warrants and their backing can be used to build a case for a claim. The acceptance of Governor LePage's executive order depends on citizens' shared assumptions, beliefs, and values and the Governor has clearly rallied for those commonalities.

In the last lesson you looked at other arguments and identified what underlying warrants linked the claims with their evidence. The short essay in lesson four about junk food in public school vending machines specifically stated its warrant: "Having healthier children is something this country values." Not all arguments, however, have explicit warrants. It is more common that they are implied. You may have found that as you reviewed the arguments in lesson four. For example, when you read the journal article about zoo animals' welfare, did you find where the author specifically stated warrants that linked her claims for re-defining zoos to take into account both human and animal needs? Or did you find that the basic assumptions (that humans having the opportunity to view "wild" animals is a good thing and that zoo animals having the right to homes that provide their basic needs, including dignity, is also a good thing) were simply implied?

Even though many writers do not explicitly state their warrants, it is a good idea for you to do so in your Toulmin essay. This will help you clearly identify what your warrants look like, how they are different from your claims, and what they might need in the way of backing, should they be warrants that are not widely known and accepted.

QUALIFIERS

As explained in lesson four, qualifiers are words or phrases that writers use to set limits on their assertions to prevent them from being deemed as applying universally. Qualifiers are probable rather than absolute. Arguments that use terms like *always, never, everyone, no one, all,* and *none* run the risk of alienating readers. Very few situations that we encounter involve absolutes. It's not a black and white world; there are many shades of gray. So you should use qualifiers, words like *often, most, sometimes, almost, for the most part,* and *typically,* to reassure the reader that you are not being authoritarian or absolutist in your argument. You want to convince the reader that you are a calm, logical, credible source of information and qualifiers help you do that. Excessive use of qualifiers, however, can result in a weak argument, so be mindful of your use of these tempering words and phrases.

As you work on your Toulmin essay, try to identify several spots where qualifiers would help strengthen your argument. These might be in cases where strong evidence is found in both your view and that of the opponent's. Qualifiers may be helpful in cases where definitive data is not available or where both sides have strong, emotionally-charged convictions. For example, sound discussions of climate change often include qualifiers, since there is so much disagreement about its extent and causes.

CONCESSIONS AND REBUTTALS

Lesson four explored the roles of concessions and rebuttals in a Toulmin argument. The concession is an opportunity to extend a hand to your opponent, to acknowledge that an opposing view is strong and irrefutable. A concession helps maintain civility of an argument and also increases your credibility as an objective, fair writer.

When you make a concession in your Toulmin argument, remember to maintain commitment to your claim. When you concede that an opposing viewpoint is valid, make sure that it is not one that would completely undermine your claim. If that is the case, you can re-assess the decision to include that concession. If you determine that the concession is something that would likely arise in discussion of this topic, you may need to re-examine your claim. You may have chosen a claim that cannot be convincingly supported and you may need to revise it somewhat.

Remember to keep your concession brief and respectful. There is no need to provide abundant detail about the concession. Simply admitting that your opponent has a valid point is sufficient. Then move on. Sometimes a concession can be stated in one sentence, with the rebuttal following in a separate sentence or sentences. Other times, the concession and rebuttal can be contained within the same sentence. In either instance, it works well to have the rebuttal follow the concession, leaving the reader with the statement that backs the writer's argument.

Here are two concessions and rebuttals taken from the junk food essay in lesson four. The first concession and rebuttal are contained in one sentence; the second concession and rebuttal are in two separate sentences. In both instances, the rebuttal is listed after the concession, so the reader carries with him/her the idea that supports the writer's claim.

While it can be said that junk food in small amounts is not harmful to children's diets **[The first part of this sentence is a Concession, recognizing a valid point of the opposition],** it remains a fact that our children are alarmingly overweight and school vending machines provide convenient opportunities for consumption of harmful foods without proper parental supervision of food choices **[The rest of the sentence refutes the opposition; it is a Rebuttal].**

Vending machines have been identified as contributing significantly to revenue-strapped school districts and some feel that removing junk food from vending machines will reduce that revenue **[This sentence is another Concession to the opposing view].** Eliminating junk food from vending machines and replacing it with healthy foods will still provide school districts revenue and children higher quality, healthier foods **[This sentence refutes the opposing view; it is a Rebuttal].**

Concessions and rebuttals go together. They work in tandem to help strengthen an argument. While rebuttals, focusing on an opposing view, may seem like something to avoid, they can actually help you as you build your Toulmin argument. Rebuttals remind you to look at your argument as a skeptic. Look for the holes that might be poked in your argument. Look for opportunities to attack your claim and to challenge its support, warrants, and backing. Anticipate your opposition and be prepared for it. You can look at your Toulmin elements and ask yourself: "Would anyone try to dispute my claim? If so, how would they do that? What points might they typically make? Would anyone challenge the underlying assumption s (warrants) of my argument? If so, what parts of my warrants and backing would be vulnerable?" Your answers to these questions can form the basis for your rebuttals.

Rebuttals, as mentioned in lesson four, are essentially mini-arguments. They may contain a claim, support, warrant, and backing. They should be built with the same care that is given your entire argument. You should be especially careful in your rebuttals that you avoid logical fallacies (discussed in lesson three). This is not always the case in political debate. Logical fallacies permeate many rebuttals, with one of the most common being the ad hominem (against the man) fallacy. This technique switches the attention from the issue to the speaker, diverting the audience's attention to personal characteristics or actions that may, in fact, have nothing to do with the topic being discussed. Take care that your rebuttals are built soundly.

Finally, when you complete your rebuttals, return the reader's focus to your claim. Don't leave the essay on a note of negativity or skepticism. Provide solid support for your rebuttal and then move on. Make your exit from the rebuttal discussion a confident and respectful one.

DOCUMENTING YOUR SOURCES

You have most likely spent some time in your college career studying the proper documentation of sources. You have studied the University's plagiarism policy. You have certified that you understand it and will comply with it. Failure to do so means jeopardizing your academic (and possibly professional) career.

Proper documentation of sources is the key to complying with this policy. It's also the way to be intellectually honest. Documentation is your way to say to the reader "These good ideas and words are not mine. I borrowed them from a fine author. Here's where you can find the author's work." Documentation is not only a way to protect you; it is also a helpful tool for the reader. If the reader is interested in the "borrowed" ideas and words you present, he/she can get more information via the information you provide in the in-text citations, works cited entry, and bibliography. (You learned earlier that checking out the bibliography of your sources is a good way to verify their reliability as well as find other source materials.)

Documentation is a helpful tool that is critical to your academic success. Knowing documentation is so important, how can you be certain you are doing it correctly? How can you recognize when it is appropriate to omit documentation and when it is essential to include it? There are some basic rules to follow. If a piece of information is part of a general body of knowledge shared by a large group of readers, it is not necessary to document it. For example, American readers know about the attacks on September 11, 2001. General statements about those attacks would not require documentation. However, specific details, details that may not be widely known by the American public, would require documentation. Using an author's words always requires documentation. Paraphrasing (putting an author's ideas in your own words) and summarizing (condensing an author's ideas and putting them in your own words) both require documentation, unless the ideas are among those items that are part of the reader's general body of knowledge.

You can protect yourself from inadvertent plagiarism by taking steps as you gather information. When you are taking notes for your research, be sure you know which ideas and words are yours and which belong to other authors. A good way to take notes is to divide the page vertically, placing the author's words/ideas in the left hand side and your reactions to those words/ideas in the right hand side. That way, as you gather info for your paper, you know where you borrowed ideas and where you responded to them.

You should also remember to use direct quotations as little as possible. The essays you write in this and other classes are to display your writing, not that of others. So try to use direct quotations only when the author's words are absolutely on target, when you have determined that you could not phrase the idea more effectively. Then, as you integrate the quote into your prose, introduce the author to your reader, place the quote, and then add your observation about the quote. That demonstrates that you are really merging the author's ideas with your own.

Lesson four discussed the importance of carefully summarizing an author's work. The summary must be fair, thorough and accurate. The same can be said for paraphrasing. When you re-word an author's ideas, be true to the source.

You are fortunate to have an assistant in your efforts to avoid plagiarism. The Turnitin website (www.turnitin.com) has helpful information and is a resource you will use to assess your paraphrasing, summarizing, quoting, and citing skills. The site compares your paper with research data and other student papers in a huge database and identifies similarities. Each essay is awarded a score based on a percentage of borrowed materials—the lower the percentage, the better.

Additional information and resources are available to you from your instructor, in the classroom, and in the APUS Library, which has a very helpful Student Academic Resource center, located under the Resources & Services tab. Included in this center are clear instructions on general principles of documentation, as well as specific guidance for documentation styles. The MLA style is covered in depth.

Don't ruin all the important work you have done on your argument paper by neglecting the documentation step. Take the time to gather information from your sources correctly, integrate that source material smoothly into your prose, and tell your reader where you found that information.

ORGANIZING A TOULMIN ARGUMENT

Once you have gathered all your source materials, determined what your claim will be, decided how you will support it, identified what qualifiers you may need to include, spelled out warrant(s) underlying your claim, listed any backing the warrant(s) may need, and explored possible concessions and rebuttals, it's time to put it all together! This is an exciting, daunting task.

How do you organize a Toulmin argument? There are a number of ways to do so. The websites you were encouraged to review in lesson four have some suggested organizational schemes. You should select a method of organization that best meets your needs, as well as the requirements of your topic and the expectations of your reader. In general, a Toulmin argument should unfold in this order:

1. Introduction

2. Background

3. Body

4. Conclusion

The key elements of support, qualifiers, warrant, backing, concession, and rebuttal can be integrated into that general pattern in a way that seems most effective to you. If you would like a more specific guideline for organizing this essay, you could try this outline:

1. Introducing the Argument

    a. Hook

    b. Problem description

    c. Claim

2. Demonstrating Support

    a. Evidence (Qualifier)

    b. Evidence (Qualifier)

    c. Evidence (Qualifier)

3. Providing Warrants

    a. Warrant (Backing)

    b. Warrant (Backing)

4. Addressing Opposition

    a. Concession(s)

    b. Rebuttal(s)

5. Concluding the Argument

    a. Claim

    b. Implications

    c. Powerful exit line

Remember to review lesson three, as it covers important principles about getting the reader into and out of your essay. You will want to get your reader engaged quickly with a vibrant introduction. You should also examine the discussion of the thesis in lesson three, as this will be the location of your claim. It is recommended that the thesis statement be placed at the end of your first paragraph. You will want to move your reader with ease from one paragraph to the next. Smooth transitions typically occur because of the flow of ideas; they can be enhanced by using specific transitional words or phrases and by repeating key terms related to your topic. Concessions and rebuttals are usually found in later parts of a Toulmin argument. Remember to present these to the reader in a manner that is civil and respectful of the opposing view. Contentious rebuttals will not be to your advantage. Your conclusion will be the finale. It will be what the reader takes with him/her from your Toulmin argument. Emphasize the claim and leave the reader with a powerful exit line. Make it memorable, truly memorable!

CONCLUSION

This completes lesson five. In this lesson you explored the Toulmin argument method in more detail, providing more specific assistance as you build your argument essay. The lesson explored types of claims typically found in these arguments (fact, problem-based, definition, evaluation, and cause) and provided additional information on the Toulmin elements of support, qualifiers, warrants, backing, concessions, and rebuttals. You also studied sources for your support, looking at ways to determine reliability of sources as well as important principles related to documenting sources used in your paper. Finally the lesson provided you suggestions on how to organize your Toulmin argument. The topics covered in this and previous lessons provide a good foundation for you to demonstrate that you can critically evaluate a piece of writing.

QUESTIONS TO CONSIDER

1. What forms do claims take and how does evidence for those claims differ?

2. How should a writer go about assessing evidence and its sources?

3. What are the benefits and possible drawbacks of using qualifiers?

4. How do warrants unify readers of a Toulmin argument?

5. Why is documentation of source materials essential?

6. What considerations should be taken into account when organizing a Toulmin argument?

Works Cited

Catt, Carrie Chapman. "Address to Congress on Women's Suffrage." U.S. Congress.

Washington, D.C. Nov. 1917. *American Rhetoric: Top 100 Speeches.* Web. 6 Jan.

2012.

Chisholm, Shirley. "For the Equal Rights Amendment." U.S. House of Representatives,

Washington, D.C. 10 Aug. 1970. *American Rhetoric: Top 100 Speeches.* Web. 6 Jan.

2012.

LePage, Paul R. "An Order Regarding the Use of Green Building Standards in State

Buildings." State of Maine. Office of Governor. 7 Dec. 2011. Web 14 Jan. 2012.

Wickins-Drazilova, Dita. "Zoo Animal Welfare*." Journal of Agricultural and Environmental

Ethics* 19.1 (2006): 27-36. *ProQuest Research Library.* Web. 6 Jan. 2012.

CHAPTER 6: USING THE ROGERIAN METHOD OF ARGUMENTATION

INTRODUCTION

This lesson introduces and explains the Rogerian strategy for writing essays, one which attempts to persuade while stressing understanding and common ground. We often think of debates in terms of pros and cons or like a court trial that emphasizes the competition of two sides in the presentation of their arguments. The classical and Toulmin argumentation strategies typically seek to win a debate through the presentation of a persuasive argument.

However, many issues do not have a clear right or wrong side to them. Even if they do, persuading an audience on the other side is difficult if not impossible if their side is presented as the wrong one. Imagine, for instance, two spouses debating where to go for a vacation. There is no right or wrong choice, and depicting one side or the other as such will not be a very effective way to persuade the other spouse.

In 1951, Carl Rogers, a psychologist, put forth the theory that the primary reason people had difficulty in resolving disputes is that the people were constantly evaluating each other. The more deeply-held or emotional a belief, the more a person would be seeking to judge and discredit another person's opposing statements, the result being a failure to truly hear or understand those statements. Roger proposed as the solution first to try to understand the other side and then to negotiate together to reach a consensus.

The Rogerian strategy of argumentation seeks to find a win-win outcome. The purpose of Rogerian argumentation is to use common ground to reach a consensus.

Essentially, the Rogerian strategy acts as a mediator between two sides, seeking to negotiate to find a common ground acceptable to both. The Rogerian strategy is most effective for those issues that are highly emotional, including many social and political problems, such as capital punishment, abortion, torture, and many more. Such issues have few simple solutions to them, and asserting or implying that the solution or answer is clear or obvious will actually make the argument seem biased and less persuasive. Generally, people do not want to be told that a value or belief they hold dear is just plain wrong.

The Rogerian strategy seeks to lessen the threatening aspect of the argument by emphasizing the value of the opposition's side and motivations. People tend to respond similarly to how they are treated, so if an argument doesn't seem to be attacking the other side, the readers on the other side are less likely to be as critical in their attack on the argument they are reading. The Rogerian strategy encourages the audience to be more open to the argument being made because the writer has already demonstrated openness and respect for the arguments on the other side of the issue.

The very idea that everyone is entitled to his or her own opinion demonstrates the need for Rogerian strategies of argumentation. The Rogerian strategy forces the writer to consider the possibility that his or her side may not be absolutely right. In other words, knowing that the argument is only the writer's opinion, the writer asserts that this opinion is a right one to have on the matter, if not the only right one, and seeks to persuade the audience also to accept the possibility that the writer's opinion is a right one, if not the only right one. The following sections will help you better understand the process of creating a Rogerian argument.

ORGANIZATION

The Rogerian strategy assumes that the audience will be highly critical if not outright hostile to the argument being presented. Readers with differing opinions from what they are reading tend to be contentious, immediately challenging each and every assertion that they find objectionable. Of course, readers should be critical in this way, but they should also be open to the possibility of changing their minds.

The Rogerian strategy seeks to lead the reader gently to the conclusion of the argument and often begins objectively by stating the problem and then appeals to the audience further by showing the benefits of the opposing side. Only then are the reasons in support of the argument described, but before the audience can become defensive, the common ground and higher interest that benefit both sides are emphasized.

The Rogerian strategy will typically follow this pattern:

1. Describe the problem

2. Show understanding and value of opposing views

3. Assert position

4. Demonstrate common ground or higher interest

For example, look at the table below. This illustrates a discussion between two spouses deciding where to go on vacation. One spouse seeks to persuade the other that Galveston is a better vacation destination than Denver. The Rogerian argument might be organized like this:

Table 6.1: Rogerian Structure of a Spousal Vacation Discussion.

Parts of Rogerian Structure	Example of the Part	Part Explained
Describe the Problem	Both trips cost roughly the same, but we have enough money in our savings for one. You want to go hiking in the mountains, which will require a plane trip to Denver. I want to visit family in Galveston, which would be a ten-hour drive.	The problem has objectively been stated, focusing only on the facts of both trips.
Show Understanding and Value of Opposing Views	The mountains are beautiful this time of year, and we haven't been hiking in a long time, so it would be great to get that kind of exercise. It would also be nice to be alone together for the vacation.	Appreciation is demonstrated for the value of a trip to Denver for its beauty, exercise, and alone time.
Assert Position	I haven't seen my family in a few years, and my father is getting on in age, so I don't know how many more chances we'll have to see him. We would have time to visit the beaches too.	Reasons supporting a trip to Galveston are presented.
Demonstrate Common Ground or Higher Interest	We could take some nice hikes on the beach, so we could have some great opportunities for exercise. We could also do some camping for a day or two to get some alone time or take a few day trips to Houston. I don't know if I'll get another chance to see my family either.	Common ground is demonstrated by mentioning the beauty of the beaches, exercise possibilities, and the option for alone time (the same reasons given for the trip to Denver). The higher interest of valuing family is noted as well.

Note, that the Rogerian strategy emphasizes "common ground," which is distinct from

"middle ground" argumentation strategy, which emphasizes finding a compromise where both sides have to give a little. For instance, a middle ground argument using this example might be to suggest that the trip be split with one week in Denver and one week in Galveston or to suggest that the trips be taken separately. (See the discussion of developing a middle ground argument in Lesson 8.)

DESCRIBE THE PROBLEM

The introduction section of a Rogerian essay presents the problem in a fair and objective way, often pointing out how everyone (the writer and reader) are affected by the issue and should want to reach a resolution. Why is the issue significant? Why does it need to be resolved? Such questions are answered in this section.

For issues that seem to be continually debated, like capital punishment or abortion, this section is a good place to explain why the best we can hope for in such debates is to reach some type of a consensus or agreement on one aspect of the matter if not the entire matter. For example, if writing about the abortion debate, the first section might note that it is impossible to know with any certainty exactly when life begins, but that we still can reach agreement on the legal rights of parents in the decision making of a pregnant teenager. It is advisable to present the issue as a problem to be solved together rather than as a debate. Framing the issue as a problem to be solved invites the audience to engage in the essay as an act of seeking a solution together rather than as a "debate." For example:

Weak:

People against torture insist it violates human rights, but people supporting torture insists it's a necessary tool to ensure people's safety.

Strong:

When it comes to the issue of torture, it is possible to protect human rights while also ensuring safety.

Both examples are objective, but the second example demonstrates that a shared larger goal between both sides is to protect people's rights and ensure their safety. Here, and throughout the essay, the writer should demonstrate as much respect as possible for the other side's goals or values.

Please note: writers who are new to the Rogerian approach should put the thesis statement/claim in the introduction paragraph so that the main idea is clear. When using the Rogerian approach, it can easily become a report about the beliefs of both sides, so a writer developing experience with the Rogerian strategy should put the thesis in the introduction to clarify that the essay will take a position on the issue.

SHOW UNDERSTANDING AND VALUE OF OPPOSING VIEWS

Next, present as fairly and objectively as possible the views of the other side. Doing so demonstrates that the issue has been fully considered without prejudice. It builds goodwill with the audience. Readers are more likely to trust writers who show respect for others' views, even when disagreeing with those views.

Explain which parts of the opposing views are strong and why. What are the underlying good values that support these views? For example:

Weak:

Many argue torture violates the rights of those terrorists who are tortured.

Strong:

Of course we must respect the rights of all people, including terrorists.

The weak example here objectively states the value embraced by the other side. However, the strong example embraces that value. The audience will be more likely to believe this writer's argument because the writer has demonstrated a shared value, a shared respect for the rights of all people.

ASSERT POSITION

After the audience sees that the writer understands and respects their opposing views, they will be more willing to listen to the writer's side and similarly attempt to understand and respect the argument being presented. This section presents the writer's side of the issue.

Be careful not to "come out swinging" in this section though! Remember the goal is not to "beat" the audience and win the debate; the goal is still to work with the audience to negotiate to a consensus together. Show the validity of the argument but continue to use respectful, neutral language. For example:

Weak:

Torture absolutely must be allowed as the only way to protect innocent lives.

Strong:

Torture can be justifiable in situations where innocent lives are directly at stake. The weak version uses language that might make the audience defensive, such as "absolutely" and "only." The strong version continues the strategy of negotiating together to reach a consensus by suggesting only that torture "can be" allowed when lives are "directly" threatened. Followed with good reasons showing situations when lives really have been directly threatened and only suggesting that torture is one possible way to protect those lives, the audience will be more likely to accept that torture just might be a good solution, if not the only solution, to protect those lives.

This section might note limitations to the argument, further demonstrating that the writer has considered the issue as fairly as possible. For example:

Weak:

We can trust our law enforcement to use torture only when it is necessary.

Strong:

There may be some members in law enforcement who might use torture unnecessarily, but safeguards can be put in place to ensure that it is used only when all other options have failed and only when lives are in immediate danger.

The weak example opens the door for an immediate objection not just to the idea of using torture but to how torture would be used. The strong example acknowledges the possible problem of using torture when it is not warranted and offers a solution. The audience may still be convinced that torture can be a justified in some situations if these safeguards exist to prevent its abuse.

Remember, the Rogerian strategy does not attempt to persuade the audience to accept the argument absolutely but to accept that the argument is a valid one at least under certain circumstances.

DEMONSTRATE COMMON GROUND OR HIGHER INTEREST

Finally, close with a focus on finding a common ground or calling for a higher interest or goal. Use this section not to ask the readers to give up their side, but to ask the readers to come together on the common ground.

Identify the goals and values that the opposition has in support of their side and show how those goals and values might be accomplished on your side as well. What shared values are found on the common ground? How might those values be respected by both sides in some way? For example:

Weak:

An innocent person's life is much more important than the rights of a terrorist.

Strong:

> If a choice must be made between an innocent person's life and the rights of a
>
> terrorist, then torture may be our only option.

The weak example asks the reader to give up the value of human rights for the terrorist,

while the strong example respects the value of those rights, but asserts that they may have

to be violated in some extreme circumstances to protect the lives of other people. The

strong example emphasizes the higher interest of protecting life and the common ground of

respect for human rights and people's lives.

This section might also be used to describe situations where the solution would work

while acknowledging that there may be other situations when the solution might not be the

best. Thus, the audience is persuaded to accept that the solution is a good one, at least in

some contexts. For example:

Weak:

> The terrorists' choice to threaten others has caused them to give up their rights, so it
>
> is perfectly justifiable to violate their rights to protect others.

Strong:

> Very few situations exist when lives are directly threatened, and only in those
>
> situations can torture be justified as a way to protect innocent lives.

The weak example asserts a belief that the audience might find objectionable and debate,

but the strong example asserts that the argument in support of torture exists primarily for

the extreme situations when lives are directly threatened, a proposition the audience may be

much more willing to accept as true.

WRITING A ROGERIAN ARGUMENT

All writing requires careful audience analysis to be effective, but the nature of the Rogerian strategy as negotiation between two sides makes such audience analysis even more important. What do the readers likely already know about the topic? What are their likely fears or objections? Why would they likely feel one side is right or wrong? What values or goals are shared with the audience?

When preparing a Rogerian argument, it might help to write a paragraph, outline, or a brief draft of an essay from the opposing side of the issue. Pretend, for a moment, that you are your opponent. How would you write the essay in support of the other side? Then, review what you've written from this opposing side. Where are there shared values or goals expressed? What points do you agree with? Try using these points to show understanding and appreciation of the other side while negotiating a common ground. (In fact, such opposition papers are often written in government organizations for the same reason of identifying mutual values and goals to later be used in policy papers or speeches that support the other side.)

Remember, be respectful and compassionate with word choice throughout the essay. Avoid absolutes like none, never, all, or always, leaving room for exceptions. Avoid words like clearly or obviously if the idea might actually be debatable to those who disagree with you. Be especially wary of rhetorical questions since they can sound sarcastic to others who do not agree with your answer to the question. For example:

Weak:

How could we not use torture if a million lives were at stake?

Strong:

Could torture make a difference if a million lives were at stake?

The audience could answer the weak question with many possible options other than torture that might be tried. The question sounds sarcastic to those who oppose the use of torture. In contrast, the strong question is open-ended; both proponents and opponents of torture might ask such a question. Seeking the answer together is the goal of the Rogerian strategy.

CONCLUSION

This completes lesson six. Hopefully, after reading this lesson, you have a better idea of how to approach a Rogerian essay. When writing an essay using the Rogerian strategy, ask yourself:

- Has the introduction fairly and objectively presented the problem?

- Are the opponents' views accurately and considerately explained?

- Are the values shared with my opponents identified?

- Is my tone compassionate and respectful?

- Is the common ground provided truly a win-win for both sides?

The checklist above should help you write an effective Rogerian argument.

QUESTIONS TO CONSIDER

1. How is the Rogerian argumentative style different than the Toulmin method?

2. Why is the Rogerian method effective for those issues that are highly emotional?

3. How important is explaining the counterargument in the Rogerian method of argumentation?

Chapter 7: Using the Rogerian Method Continued

Introduction

In lesson six, you learned about the Rogerian argumentative style of writing. Lesson seven will review this style of writing again through the examination of two famous examples of this argumentative style: President Obama's DNC speech given in 2008 and President Reagan's RNC speech given in 1980.

Rogerian Argumentative Review

Remember that the Rogerian strategy of argumentation does not seek to win a debate but instead seeks to prove a claim through an understanding of the other side and a discussion of shared values. In other words, with the Rogerian style of argumentation, a writer must first make a claim about an issue. Then, in order to prove this claim, that writer needs to demonstrate a clear understanding of the other side of this issue and find the common ground between both sides. This common ground is used to prove the writer's claim. This strategy encourages the audience to be more open to the argument being made because the writer has demonstrated respect for other arguments about an issue.

Rogerian Sample Argument - President Obama's DNC Acceptance Speech, 2008

Our first stop in this week's lesson is to review a Rogerian sample argument, President Obama's DNC Acceptance Speech in 2008. Please click on the following link to listen to the Acceptance Speech: <u>The American Promise</u>. You may also read the <u>acceptance speech</u> given by President Obama below at the end of this lesson. This discussion will not focus on the topics that Obama presents in his speech, but the way in which Obama organizes his speech. When you listen to or read this speech, note that there is an argument that President Obama makes – he wants to prove to the audience that he is the best candidate. However, to do this, he needs to ensure that the other side, made up of Republican voters, is not alienated by his discussion. Therefore, his acceptance speech cannot be confrontational. Instead, he must attempt to prove his side by considering the views of Republicans and Independents and showing the common ground.

Let's take a look at the speech in further detail. First, the purpose of Obama's speech is not only to accept the democratic nomination for president, but also to convince voters to vote for him. However, President Obama not only wants to convince Democrats to vote for him, he also seeks Republican votes. Therefore, when he opens his speech, he does not 'attack' the views of the Republicans. Instead, he opens with a dream that holds true for all Americans: "It is that promise that has always set this country apart - that through hard work and sacrifice, each of us can pursue our individual dreams but still come together as one American family, to ensure that the next generation can pursue their dreams as well." Then, instead of insulting the Republican candidate, John McCain, he praises him: "Now let there be no doubt. The Republican nominee, John McCain, has worn the uniform of our country with bravery and distinction, and for that we owe him our gratitude and respect." In this way, Obama keeps the views of his audience in mind. Remember from lesson six that the Rogerian strategy appeals to the audience by showing the benefits of the opposing side. The audience would not be swayed to vote for Obama if he insults their beliefs or their candidate.

In the body of the speech, Obama begins to give the meat to his side, the reasons in support of his argument. He first lists some of the issues that American faced in 2008. Then, he explains how his policies differ from McCain's. In this section, he carefully avoids insulting McCain. Instead, Obama shows how McCain is mistaken. However, he does so in a manner that unifies all Americans, no matter what their political affiliation is: "Tonight, I say to the American people, to Democrats and Republicans and Independents across this great land - enough! This moment - this election - is our chance to keep, in the 21st century, the American promise alive." As illustrated in Obama's speech, in a Rogerian essay, it is important to keep the audience in mind throughout the argument, even when presenting your particular argument.

Lesson six mentioned that at the end of a Rogerian essay, the common ground and higher interest benefiting both sides should be emphasized. President Obama does this at the closing of his speech:

> [L]et us agree that patriotism has no party. I love this country, and so do you, and so does John McCain. The men and women who serve in our battlefields may be Democrats and Republicans and Independents, but they have fought together and bled together and some died together under the same proud flag. They have not served a Red America or a Blue America - they have served the United States of America. [...]
>
> We may not agree on abortion, but surely we can agree on reducing the number of unwanted pregnancies in this country. The reality of gun ownership may be different for hunters in rural Ohio than for those plagued by gang-violence in Cleveland, but don't tell me we can't uphold the Second Amendment while keeping AK-47s out of the hands of criminals. I know there are differences on same-sex marriage, but surely we can agree that our gay and lesbian brothers and sisters deserve to visit the person they love in the hospital and to live lives free of

discrimination. Passions fly on immigration, but I don't know anyone who benefits

when a mother is separated from her infant child or an employer undercuts American

wages by hiring illegal workers. This too is part of America's promise - the promise of

a democracy where we can find the strength and grace to bridge divides and unite in

common effort.

In this section, Obama attempts to bridge the gap and establish the common ground

between Republicans and Democrats. He shows that all Americans want the best for the

United States, and he also attempts to show the common ground between a number of

ethical issues. This section of the speech illustrates what is meant by common ground.

ROGERIAN SAMPLE ARGUMENT - PRESIDENT REAGAN'S RNC ACCEPTANCE SPEECH, 1980

Of course, Barrack Obama was not the only president who made use of the Rogerian

style of argumentation. Ronald Reagan did the same with his Republican National

Convention speech in 1980. Please click here to listen to this speech, which starts at about

3:15 into the video: President Reagan's RNC Acceptance Speech. You can also find his

speech at the end of this lesson as well. Like the section above that discussed Obama's

acceptance speech, this section emphasizes the organization of Reagan's speech, not the

particular topics within his speech. In this speech, Reagan's goal is similar to Obama's 2008

speech: he too wants to win the votes of Americans. To do this, Reagan utilizes the Rogerian

format.

First, Reagan begins his speech by removing the barriers between Republicans and

Democrats. He states this directly at the beginning of his speech:

> I want my candidacy to unify our country, to renew the American spirit and sense of
>
> purpose. I want to carry our message to every American, regardless of party
>
> affiliation, who is a member of this community of shared values.

In this quotation, Reagan does not polarize his audience. He is keeping his audience in mind, and he lets his audience know that his speech and candidacy is for all Americans, not just for one political group. In the introduction, he also tells his audience that all Americans share the same concerns:

> Never before in our history have Americans been called upon to face three grave
>
> threats to our very existence, any one of which could destroy us. We face a
>
> disintegrating economy, a weakened defense and an energy policy based on the
>
> sharing of scarcity.

This quotation from Reagan shows that all Americans, no matter what their political affiliation is, share the same concerns. Rogerian arguments do not start by honing in on the argument and antagonizing the other side. Instead, like the example above from Reagan's speech, Rogerian arguments should appeal to both sides of an issue.

In the body of his speech, Reagan continues his argument in a calm, rational manner. Reagan shows the flaws with the other candidate; however, he avoids insulting the other side, and instead, Reagan explains why his beliefs are stronger than the other candidate. He does this through specific points that illustrate unity between Americans: "Together, let us make this a new beginning. Let us make a commitment to care for the needy; to teach our children the values and the virtues handed down to us by our families; to have the courage to defend those values and the willingness to sacrifice for them." Reagan also unifies Americans in his speech with the following: "It's time to put America back to work, to make our cities and towns resound with the confident voices of men and women of all races, nationalities and faiths bringing home to their families a paycheck they can cash

for honest money." Reagan does this in his speech because he wants the other side to vote

for him, so he attempts to create a tone of unity, not division.

Finally, at the end of his argument, President Reagan shows the common ground

between all American voters:

> It is impossible to capture in words the splendor of this vast continent which
> God has granted as our portion of His creation. There are no words to express the
> extraordinary strength and character of this breed of people we call Americans.

> Everywhere we've met thousands of Democrats, Independents and
> Republicans from all economic conditions, walks of life bound together in that
> community of shared values of family, work, neighborhood, peace and freedom. They
> are concerned, yes, they're not frightened. They're disturbed, but not dismayed. They
> are the kind of men and women Tom Paine had in mind when he wrote, during the
> darkest days of the American Revolution, "We have it in our power to begin the world
> over again."

In Reagan's final section of his speech, he establishes the common ground between all

Americans by showing that Americans share the same issues and the same values. Like

President Obama above, President Reagan shows that all Americans want the best for the

United States. In this final section, Reagan, like Obama, illustrates how finding the common

ground between political parties can help strengthen an argument and a politician to be

elected.

CONCLUSION

In this lesson you read two examples of successful Rogerian arguments. Often,

politicians use the Rogerian strategy in order to win over voters. Using Rogerian win-win strategy appeals to audiences, and, at least in the case of Barrack Obama and Ronald Reagan, helps to persuade an audience. Just like the Rogerian argument helps politicians win elections, the Rogerian argumentative method can help you successfully persuade an audience as well.

QUESTIONS TO CONSIDER

1. Why would politicians consider the Rogerian method useful?

2. How can reading Rogerian arguments help strengthen your argumentative skills?

3. Why is it important to consider the values of your audience when forming an argument?

Works Cited

Obama, Barack. "The American Promise." *American Rhetoric.* n.d. Web. Jan. 6, 2012.

Reagan, Ronald. "Acceptance of Republican Nomination for President at the 1980

Republican National Convention in Detroit, Michigan." *American Experience.* PBS.

WGBH Educational Foundation. n.d. Web. Jan. 6, 2012.

READING SELECTIONS

Remarks of Senator Barack Obama –"The American Promise" -Democratic National Convention

August 28, 2008

Denver, Colorado

As prepared for delivery

To Chairman Dean and my great friend Dick Durbin; and to all my fellow citizens of this great nation;

With profound gratitude and great humility, I accept your nomination for the presidency of the United States.

.

Let me express my thanks to the historic slate of candidates who accompanied me on this journey, and especially the one who traveled the farthest - a champion for working Americans and an inspiration to my daughters and to yours -- Hillary Rodham Clinton. To President Clinton, who last night made the case for change as only he can make it; to Ted Kennedy, who embodies the spirit of service; and to the next Vice President of the United States, Joe Biden, I thank you. I am grateful to finish this journey with one of the finest statesmen of our time, a man at ease with everyone from world leaders to the conductors on the Amtrak train he still takes home every night.

To the love of my life, our next First Lady, Michelle Obama, and to Sasha and Malia - I love you so much, and I'm so proud of all of you.

Four years ago, I stood before you and told you my story - of the brief union between a young man from Kenya and a young woman from Kansas who weren't well-off or well-known, but shared a belief that in America, their son could achieve whatever he put his mind to.

It is that promise that has always set this country apart - that through hard work and sacrifice, each of us can pursue our individual dreams but still come together as one American family, to ensure that the next generation can pursue their dreams as well.

That's why I stand here tonight. Because for two hundred and thirty two years, at each moment when that promise was in jeopardy, ordinary men and women - students and soldiers, farmers and teachers, nurses and janitors -- found the courage to keep it alive.

We meet at one of those defining moments - a moment when our nation is at war, our economy is in turmoil, and the American promise has been threatened once more.

Tonight, more Americans are out of work and more are working harder for less. More of you have lost your homes and even more are watching your home values plummet. More of you have cars you can't afford to drive, credit card bills you can't afford to pay, and tuition that's beyond your reach.

These challenges are not all of government's making. But the failure to respond is a direct result of a broken politics in Washington and the failed policies of George W. Bush.

America, we are better than these last eight years. We are a better country than this.

This country is more decent than one where a woman in Ohio, on the brink of retirement, finds herself one illness away from disaster after a lifetime of hard work.

This country is more generous than one where a man in Indiana has to pack up the equipment he's worked on for twenty years and watch it shipped off to China, and then chokes up as he explains how he felt like a failure when he went home to tell his family the news.

We are more compassionate than a government that lets veterans sleep on our streets and families slide into poverty; that sits on its hands while a major American city drowns before our eyes.

Tonight, I say to the American people, to Democrats and Republicans and Independents across this great land - enough! This moment - this election - is our chance to keep, in the 21st century, the American promise alive. Because next week, in Minnesota, the same party that brought you two terms of George Bush and Dick Cheney will ask this country for a third. And we are here because we love this country too much to let the next four years look like the last eight. On November 4th, we must stand up and say: "Eight is enough."

Now let there be no doubt. The Republican nominee, John McCain, has worn the uniform of our country with bravery and distinction, and for that we owe him our gratitude and respect. And next week, we'll also hear about those occasions when he's broken with his party as evidence that he can deliver the change that we need.

But the record's clear: John McCain has voted with George Bush ninety percent of the time. Senator McCain likes to talk about judgment, but really, what does it say about your judgment when you think George Bush has been right more than ninety percent of the time? I don't know about you, but I'm not ready to take a ten percent chance on change.

The truth is, on issue after issue that would make a difference in your lives - on health care and education and the economy - Senator McCain has been anything but independent. He said that our economy has made "great progress" under this President. He said that the fundamentals of the economy are strong. And when one of his chief advisors - the man who wrote his economic plan - was talking about the anxiety Americans are feeling, he said that we were just suffering from a "mental recession," and that we've become, and I quote, "a nation of whiners."

A nation of whiners? Tell that to the proud auto workers at a Michigan plant who, after they found out it was closing, kept showing up every day and working as hard as ever, because they knew there were people who counted on the brakes that they made. Tell that to the military families who shoulder their burdens silently as they watch their loved ones leave for their third or fourth or fifth tour of duty. These are not whiners. They work hard and give back and keep going without complaint. These are the Americans that I know.

Now, I don't believe that Senator McCain doesn't care what's going on in the lives of Americans. I just think he doesn't know. Why else would he define middle-class as someone making under five million dollars a year? How else could he propose hundreds of billions in tax breaks for big corporations and oil companies but not one penny of tax relief to more than one hundred million Americans? How else could he offer a health care plan that would actually tax people's benefits, or an education plan that would do nothing to help families pay for college, or a plan that would privatize Social Security and gamble your retirement?

It's not because John McCain doesn't care. It's because John McCain doesn't get it.

For over two decades, he's subscribed to that old, discredited Republican philosophy - give more and more to those with the most and hope that prosperity trickles down to everyone else. In Washington, they call this the Ownership Society, but what it really means is – you're on your own. Out of work? Tough luck. No health care? The market will fix it. Born into poverty? Pull yourself up by your own bootstraps - even if you don't have boots. You're on your own.

Well it's time for them to own their failure. It's time for us to change America.

You see, we Democrats have a very different measure of what constitutes progress in this country.

We measure progress by how many people can find a job that pays the mortgage; whether you can put a little extra money away at the end of each month so you can someday watch your child receive her college diploma. We measure progress in the 23 million new jobs that were created when Bill Clinton was President - when the average American family saw its income go up $7,500 instead of down $2,000 like it has under George Bush.

We measure the strength of our economy not by the number of billionaires we have or the profits of the Fortune 500, but by whether someone with a good idea can take a risk and start a new business, or whether the waitress who lives on tips can take a day off to look after a sick kid without losing her job - an economy that honors the dignity of work.

The fundamentals we use to measure economic strength are whether we are living up to that fundamental promise that has made this country great - a promise that is the only reason I am standing here tonight.

Because in the faces of those young veterans who come back from Iraq and Afghanistan, I see my grandfather, who signed up after Pearl Harbor, marched in Patton's Army, and was rewarded by a grateful nation with the chance to go to college on the GI Bill.

In the face of that young student who sleeps just three hours before working the night shift, I think about my mom, who raised my sister and me on her own while she worked and earned her degree; who once turned to food stamps but was still able to send us to the best schools in the country with the help of student loans and scholarships.

When I listen to another worker tell me that his factory has shut down, I remember all those men and women on the South Side of Chicago who I stood by and fought for two decades ago after the local steel plant closed.

And when I hear a woman talk about the difficulties of starting her own business, I think about my grandmother, who worked her way up from the secretarial pool to middle-management, despite years of being passed over for promotions because she was a woman. She's the one who taught me about hard work. She's the one who put off buying a new car or a new dress for herself so that I could have a better life. She poured everything she had into me. And although she can no longer travel, I know that she's watching tonight, and that tonight is her night as well.

I don't know what kind of lives John McCain thinks that celebrities lead, but this has been mine. These are my heroes. Theirs are the stories that shaped me. And it is on their behalf that I intend to win this election and keep our promise alive as President of the United States.

What is that promise?

It's a promise that says each of us has the freedom to make of our own lives what we will, but that we also have the obligation to treat each other with dignity and respect.

It's a promise that says the market should reward drive and innovation and generate growth, but that businesses should live up to their responsibilities to create American jobs, look out for American workers, and play by the rules of the road.

Ours is a promise that says government cannot solve all our problems, but what it should do is that which we cannot do for ourselves - protect us from harm and provide every child a decent education; keep our water clean and our toys safe; invest in new schools and new roads and new science and technology.

Our government should work for us, not against us. It should help us, not hurt us. It should ensure opportunity not just for those with the most money and influence, but for every American who's willing to work.

That's the promise of America - the idea that we are responsible for ourselves, but that we also rise or fall as one nation; the fundamental belief that I am my brother's keeper; I am my sister's keeper.

That's the promise we need to keep. That's the change we need right now. So let me spell out exactly what that change would mean if I am President.

.

Change means a tax code that doesn't reward the lobbyists who wrote it, but the American workers and small businesses who deserve it.

Unlike John McCain, I will stop giving tax breaks to corporations that ship jobs overseas, and I will start giving them to companies that create good jobs right here in America.

I will eliminate capital gains taxes for the small businesses and the start-ups that will create the high-wage, high-tech jobs of tomorrow.

I will cut taxes - cut taxes - for 95% of all working families. Because in an economy like this, the last thing we should do is raise taxes on the middle-class.

And for the sake of our economy, our security, and the future of our planet, I will set a clear goal as President: in ten years, we will finally end our dependence on oil from the Middle East.

Washington's been talking about our oil addiction for the last thirty years, and John McCain has been there for twenty-six of them. In that time, he's said no to higher fuel-efficiency standards for cars, no to investments in renewable energy, no to renewable fuels. And today, we import triple the amount of oil as the day that Senator McCain took office.

Now is the time to end this addiction, and to understand that drilling is a stop-gap measure, not a long-term solution. Not even close.

As President, I will tap our natural gas reserves, invest in clean coal technology, and find ways to safely harness nuclear power. I'll help our auto companies re-tool, so that the fuel-efficient cars of the future are built right here in America. I'll make it easier for the American people to afford these new cars. And I'll invest 150 billion dollars over the next decade in affordable, renewable sources of energy   wind power and solar power and the next generation of biofuels; an investment that will lead to new industries and five million new jobs that pay well and can't ever be outsourced.

America, now is not the time for small plans.

Now is the time to finally meet our moral obligation to provide every child a world-class education, because it will take nothing less to compete in the global economy. Michelle and I are only here tonight because we were given a chance at an education. And I will not settle for an America where some kids don't have that chance. I'll invest in early childhood education. I'll recruit an army of new teachers, and pay them higher salaries and give them more support. And in exchange, I'll ask for higher standards and more accountability. And we will keep our promise to every young American - if you commit to serving your community or your country, we will make sure you can afford a college education.

Now is the time to finally keep the promise of affordable, accessible health care for every single American. If you have health care, my plan will lower your premiums. If you don't, you'll be able to get the same kind of coverage that members of Congress give themselves. And as someone who watched my mother argue with insurance companies while she lay in bed dying of cancer, I will make certain those companies stop discriminating against those who are sick and need care the most.

Now is the time to help families with paid sick days and better family leave, because nobody in America should have to choose between keeping their jobs and caring for a sick child or ailing parent.

Now is the time to change our bankruptcy laws, so that your pensions are protected ahead of CEO bonuses; and the time to protect Social Security for future generations.

And now is the time to keep the promise of equal pay for an equal day's work, because I want my daughters to have exactly the same opportunities as your sons.

Now, many of these plans will cost money, which is why I've laid out how I'll pay for every dime - by closing corporate loopholes and tax havens that don't help America grow. But I will also go through the federal budget, line by line, eliminating programs that no longer work and making the ones we do need work better and cost less - because we cannot meet twenty-first century challenges with a twentieth century bureaucracy.

And Democrats, we must also admit that fulfilling America's promise will require more than just money. It will require a renewed sense of responsibility from each of us to recover what John F. Kennedy called our "intellectual and moral strength." Yes, government must lead on energy independence, but each of us must do our part to make our homes and businesses more efficient. Yes, we must provide more ladders to success for young men who fall into lives of crime and despair. But we must also admit that programs alone can't replace parents; that government can't turn off the television and make a child do her homework; that fathers must take more responsibility for providing the love and guidance their children need.

Individual responsibility and mutual responsibility – that's the essence of America's promise.

And just as we keep our keep our promise to the next generation here at home, so must we keep America's promise abroad. If John McCain wants to have a debate about who has the temperament, and judgment, to serve as the next Commander-in-Chief, that's a debate I'm ready to have.

For while Senator McCain was turning his sights to Iraq just days after 9/11, I stood up and opposed this war, knowing that it would distract us from the real threats we face. When John McCain said we could just "muddle through" in Afghanistan, I argued for more resources and more troops to finish the fight against the terrorists who actually attacked us on 9/11, and made clear that we must take out Osama bin Laden and his lieutenants if we have them in our sights. John McCain likes to say that he'll follow bin Laden to the Gates of Hell - but he won't even go to the cave where he lives.

And today, as my call for a time frame to remove our troops from Iraq has been echoed by the Iraqi government and even the Bush Administration, even after we learned that Iraq has a $79 billion surplus while we're wallowing in deficits, John McCain stands alone in his stubborn refusal to end a misguided war.

That's not the judgment we need. That won't keep America safe. We need a President who can face the threats of the future, not keep grasping at the ideas of the past.

You don't defeat a terrorist network that operates in eighty countries by occupying Iraq. You don't protect Israel and deter Iran just by talking tough in Washington. You can't truly stand up for Georgia when you've strained our oldest alliances. If John McCain wants to follow George Bush with more tough talk and bad strategy, that is his choice - but it is not the change we need.

We are the party of Roosevelt. We are the party of Kennedy. So don't tell me that Democrats won't defend this country. Don't tell me that Democrats won't keep us safe. The Bush-McCain foreign policy has squandered the legacy that generations of Americans -- Democrats and Republicans - have built, and we are here to restore that legacy.

As Commander-in-Chief, I will never hesitate to defend this nation, but I will only send our troops into harm's way with a clear mission and a sacred commitment to give them the equipment they need in battle and the care and benefits they deserve when they come home.

I will end this war in Iraq responsibly, and finish the fight against al Qaeda and the Taliban in Afghanistan. I will rebuild our military to meet future conflicts. But I will also renew the tough, direct diplomacy that can prevent Iran from obtaining nuclear weapons and curb Russian aggression. I will build new partnerships to defeat the threats of the 21st century: terrorism and nuclear proliferation; poverty and genocide; climate change and disease. And I will restore our moral standing, so that America is once again that last, best hope for all who are called to the cause of freedom, who long for lives of peace, and who yearn for a better future.

These are the policies I will pursue. And in the weeks ahead, I look forward to debating them with John McCain.

But what I will not do is suggest that the Senator takes his positions for political purposes. Because one of the things that we have to change in our politics is the idea that people cannot disagree without challenging each other's character and patriotism.

The times are too serious; the stakes are too high for this same partisan playbook. So let us agree that patriotism has no party. I love this country, and so do you, and so does John McCain. The men and women who serve in our battlefields may be Democrats and Republicans and Independents, but they have fought together and bled together and some died together under the same proud flag. They have not served a Red America or a Blue America - they have served the United States of America.

So I've got news for you, John McCain. We all put our country first.

America, our work will not be easy. The challenges we face require tough choices, and Democrats as well as Republicans will need to cast off the worn-out ideas and politics of the past. For part of what has been lost these past eight years can't just be measured by lost wages or bigger trade deficits. What has also been lost is our sense of common purpose - our sense of higher purpose. And that's what we have to restore.

We may not agree on abortion, but surely we can agree on reducing the number of unwanted pregnancies in this country. The reality of gun ownership may be different for hunters in rural Ohio than for those plagued by gang-violence in Cleveland, but don't tell me we can't uphold the Second Amendment while keeping AK-47s out of the hands of criminals. I know there are differences on same-sex marriage, but surely we can agree that our gay and lesbian brothers and sisters deserve to visit the person they love in the hospital and to live lives free of discrimination. Passions fly on immigration, but I don't know anyone who benefits when a mother is separated from her infant child or an employer undercuts American wages by hiring illegal workers. This too is part of America's promise - the promise of a democracy where we can find the strength and grace to bridge divides and unite in common effort.

I know there are those who dismiss such beliefs as happy talk. They claim that our insistence on something larger, something firmer and more honest in our public life is just a Trojan Horse for higher taxes and the abandonment of traditional values. And that's to be expected. Because if you don't have any fresh ideas, then you use stale tactics to scare the voters. If you don't have a record to run on, then you paint your opponent as someone people should run from.

You make a big election about small things.

And you know what – it's worked before. Because it feeds into the cynicism we all have about government. When Washington doesn't work, all its promises seem empty. If your hopes have been dashed again and again, then it's best to stop hoping, and settle for what you already know.

I get it. I realize that I am not the likeliest candidate for this office. I don't fit the typical pedigree, and I haven't spent my career in the halls of Washington.

But I stand before you tonight because all across America something is stirring. What the nay-sayers don't understand is that this election has never been about me. It's been about you.

For eighteen long months, you have stood up, one by one, and said enough to the politics of the past. You understand that in this election, the greatest risk we can take is to try the same old politics with the same old players and expect a different result. You have shown what history teaches us - that at defining moments like this one, the change we need doesn't come from Washington. Change comes to Washington. Change happens because the American people demand it - because they rise up and insist on new ideas and new leadership, a new politics for a new time.

America, this is one of those moments.

I believe that as hard as it will be, the change we need is coming. Because I've seen it. Because I've lived it. I've seen it in Illinois, when we provided health care to more children and moved more families from welfare to work. I've seen it in Washington, when we worked across party lines to open up government and hold lobbyists more accountable, to give better care for our veterans and keep nuclear weapons out of terrorist hands.

And I've seen it in this campaign. In the young people who voted for the first time, and in those who got involved again after a very long time. In the Republicans who never thought they'd pick up a Democratic ballot, but did. I've seen it in the workers who would rather cut their hours back a day than see their friends lose their jobs, in the soldiers who re-enlist after losing a limb, in the good neighbors who take a stranger in when a hurricane strikes and the floodwaters rise.

This country of ours has more wealth than any nation, but that's not what makes us rich. We have the most powerful military on Earth, but that's not what makes us strong. Our universities and our culture are the envy of the world, but that's not what keeps the world coming to our shores.

Instead, it is that American spirit - that American promise - that pushes us forward even when the path is uncertain; that binds us together in spite of our differences; that makes us fix our eye not on what is seen, but what is unseen, that better place around the bend.

That promise is our greatest inheritance. It's a promise I make to my daughters when I tuck them in at night, and a promise that you make to yours - a promise that has led immigrants to cross oceans and pioneers to travel west; a promise that led workers to picket lines, and women to reach for the ballot.

And it is that promise that forty five years ago today, brought Americans from every corner of this land to stand together on a Mall in Washington, before Lincoln's Memorial, and hear a young preacher from Georgia speak of his dream.

The men and women who gathered there could've heard many things. They could've heard words of anger and discord. They could've been told to succumb to the fear and frustration of so many dreams deferred.

But what the people heard instead - people of every creed and color, from every walk of life - is that in America, our destiny is inextricably linked. That together, our dreams can be one.

"We cannot walk alone," the preacher cried. "And as we walk, we must make the pledge that we shall always march ahead. We cannot turn back."

America, we cannot turn back. Not with so much work to be done. Not with so many children to educate, and so many veterans to care for. Not with an economy to fix and cities to rebuild and farms to save. Not with so many families to protect and so many lives to mend. America, we cannot turn back. We cannot walk alone. At this moment, in this election, we must pledge once more to march into the future. Let us keep that promise - that American promise - and in the words of Scripture hold firmly, without wavering, to the hope that we confess.

Thank you, God Bless you, and God Bless the United States of America.

Acceptance of Republican Nomination for President at the 1980 Republican National Convention in Detroit, Michigan

July 17, 1980

Mr. Chairman, Mr. Vice President-to-be, this convention, my fellow citizens of this great nation:

With a deep awareness of the responsibility conferred by your trust, I accept your nomination for the presidency of the United States. I do so with deep gratitude. And I think also I might interject on behalf of all of us our thanks to Detroit and the people of Michigan and to this city for the warm hospitality we've enjoyed. And I thank you for your wholehearted response to my recommendation in regard to George Bush as a candidate for vice president.

I am very proud of our party tonight. This convention has shown to all America a party united, with positive programs for solving the nation's problems, a party ready to build a new consensus with all those across the land who share a community of values embodied in these words: family, work, neighborhood, peace and freedom.

Now I know we have had a quarrel or two but only as to the method of attaining a goal. There was no argument about the goal. As president, I will establish a liaison with the 50 governors to encourage them to eliminate, where it exists, discrimination against women. I will monitor federal laws to ensure their implementation and to add statutes if they are needed.

More than anything else, I want my candidacy to unify our country; to renew the American spirit and sense of purpose. I want to carry our message to every American, regardless of party affiliation, who is a member of this community of shared values.

Never before in our history have Americans been called upon to face three grave threats to our very existence, any one of which could destroy us. We face a disintegrating economy, a weakened defense and an energy policy based on the sharing of scarcity.

The major issue of this campaign is the direct political, personal and moral responsibility of Democratic Party leadership -- in the White House and in Congress -- for this unprecedented calamity which has befallen us. They tell us they have done the most that humanly could be done. They say that the United States has had its day in the sun, that our nation has passed its zenith. They expect you to tell your children that the American people no longer have the will to cope with their problems; that the future will be one of sacrifice and few opportunities.

My fellow citizens, I utterly reject that view. The American people, the most generous on earth, who created the highest standard of living, are not going to accept the notion that we can only make a better world for others by moving backwards ourselves. Those who believe we can have no business leading the nation.

I will not stand by and watch this great country destroy itself under mediocre leadership that drifts from one crisis to the next, eroding our national will and purpose. We have come together here because the American people deserve better from those to whom they entrust our nation's highest offices, and we stand united in our resolve to do something about it.

We need rebirth of the American tradition of leadership at every level of government and in private life as well. The United States of America is unique in world history because it has a genius for leaders -- many leaders, on many levels. But back in 1976, Mr. Carter said, "Trust me." And a lot of people did. And now, many of those people are out of work. Many have seen their savings eaten away by inflation. Many others on fixed incomes, especially the elderly, have watched helplessly as the cruel tax of inflation wasted away their purchasing power. And, today, a great many who trusted Mr. Carter wonder if we can survive the Carter policies of national defense.

"Trust me" government asks that we concentrate our hopes and dreams on one man; that we trust him to do what's best for us. But my view of government places trust not in one person or one party, but in those values that transcend persons and parties. The trust is where it belongs -- in the people. The responsibility to live up to that trust is where it belongs, in their elected leaders. That kind of relationship, between the people and their elected leaders, is a special kind of compact.

Three hundred and sixty years ago, in 1620, a group of families dared to cross a mighty ocean to build a future for themselves in a new world. When they arrived at Plymouth, Massachusetts, they formed what they called a "compact," an agreement among themselves to build a community and abide by its laws.

The single act -- the voluntary binding together of free people to live under the law -- set the pattern for what was to come.

A century and a half later, the descendants of those people pledged their lives, their fortunes and their sacred honor to found this nation. Some forfeited their fortunes and their lives; none sacrificed honor.

Four score and seven years later, Abraham Lincoln called upon the people of all America to renew their dedication and their commitment to a government of, for and by the people.

Isn't it once again time to renew our compact of freedom; to pledge to each other all that is best in our lives; all that gives meaning to them -- for the sake of this, our beloved and blessed land?

Together, let us make this a new beginning. Let us make a commitment to care for the needy; to teach our children the values and the virtues handed down to us by our families; to have the courage to defend those values and the willingness to sacrifice for them.

Let us pledge to restore, in our time, the American spirit of voluntary service, of cooperation, of private and community initiative; a spirit that flows like a deep and mighty river through the history of our nation.

As your nominee, I pledge to restore to the Federal Government the capacity to do the people's work without dominating their lives. I pledge to you a Government that will not only work well but wisely; its ability to act tempered by prudence, and its willingness to do good balanced by the knowledge that government is never more dangerous than when our desire to have it help us blinds us to its great power to harm us.

The first Republican president once said, "While the people retain their virtue and their vigilance, no administration by any extreme of wickedness or folly can seriously injure the government in the short space of four years." If Mr. Lincoln could see what's happened in these last three and a half years, he might hedge a little on that statement. But with the virtues that our legacy as a free people and with the vigilance that sustains liberty, we still have time to use our renewed compact to overcome the injuries that have been done to America these past three and a half years.

First, we must overcome something the present Administration has cooked up: a new and altogether indigestible economic stew, one part inflation, one part high unemployment, one part recession, one part runaway taxes, one part deficit spending and seasoned by an energy crisis. It's an economic stew that has turned the national stomach.

Ours are not problems of abstract economic theory. Those are problems of flesh and blood; problems that cause pain and destroy the moral fiber of real people who should not suffer the further indignity of being told by the government that it is all somehow their fault. We do not have inflation because -- as Mr. Carter says -- we've lived too well.

The head of a government which has utterly refused to live within its means and which has, in the last few days, told us that this year's deficit will be $60 billion, dares to point the finger of blame at business and labor, both of which have been engaged in a losing struggle just trying to stay even.

High taxes, we are told, are somehow good for us, as if, when government spends our money it isn't inflationary, but when we spend it, it is. Those who preside over the worst energy shortage in our history tell us to use less, so that we will run out of oil, gasoline, and natural gas a little more slowly.

Well now, conservation is desirable, of course, for we must not waste energy. But conservation is not the sole answer to our energy needs. America must get to work producing more energy. The Republican program for solving economic problems is based on growth and productivity. Large amounts of oil and natural gas lay beneath our land and off our shores, untouched because the present administration seems to believe the American people would rather see more regulation, taxes and controls than more energy.

Coal offers great potential. So does nuclear energy, produced under rigorous safety standards. It could supply electricity for thousands of industries and millions of jobs and homes. It must not be thwarted by a tiny minority opposed to economic growth which often finds friendly ears in regulatory agencies for its obstructionist campaigns. Now make no mistake. We will not permit the safety of our people or our environmental heritage to be jeopardized, but we are going to reaffirm that the economic prosperity of our people is a fundamental part of our environment.

Our problems are both acute and chronic, yet all we hear from those in positions of leadership are the same tired proposals for more government tinkering, more meddling and more control -- all of which led us to this state in the first place. Can anyone look at the record of this administration and say, "Well done"?

Can anyone compare the state of our economy when the Carter Administration took office with where we are today and say, "Keep up the good work"? Can anyone look at our reduced standing in the world today and say, "Let's have four more years of this"? I believe the American people are going to answer these questions the first week of November and their answer will be, "No – we've had enough."

And, then it will be up to us – beginning next January 20 – to offer an administration and congressional leadership of competence and more than a little courage. We must have the clarity of vision to see the difference between what is essential and what is merely desirable; and then the courage to bring our Government back under control and make it acceptable to the people. It is essential that we maintain both the forward momentum of economic growth and the strength of the safety net beneath those in society who need help. We also believe it is essential that the integrity of all aspects of Social Security are preserved.

Beyond these essentials, I believe it is clear our federal government is overgrown and overweight. Indeed, it is time for our government to go on a diet. Therefore, my first act as chief executive will be to impose an immediate and thorough freeze on Federal hiring. Then, we are going to enlist the very best minds from business, labor and whatever quarter to conduct a detailed review of every department, bureau and agency that lives by Federal appropriation.

We are also going to enlist the help and ideas of many dedicated and hard working Government employees at all levels who want a more efficient Government as much as the rest of us do. I know that many are demoralized by the confusion and waste they confront in their work as a result of failed and failing policies. Our instructions to the groups we enlist will be simple and direct. We will remind them that Government programs exist at the sufferance of the American taxpayer and are paid for with money earned by working men and women. Any program that represents a waste of their money -- a theft from their pocketbooks must have that waste eliminated or the program must go. It must go by Executive Order where possible, by Congressional action where necessary. Everything that can be run more effectively by state and local government we shall turn over to state and local government, along with the funding sources to pay for it. We are going to put an end to the money merry-go-round where our money becomes Washington's money, to be spent by the states and cities exactly the way the Federal bureaucrats tell them to. I will not accept the excuse that the Federal Government has grown so big and powerful that it is beyond the control of any President, any administration or Congress. We are going to put an end to the notion that the American taxpayer exists to fund the federal government.

The Federal Government exists to serve the American people. On January 20, we are going to re-establish that truth. Also on that date we are going to initiate action to get substantial relief for our taxpaying citizens and action to put people back to work. None of this will be based on any new form of monetary tinkering or fiscal sleight-of-hand. We will simply apply to government the common sense we all use in our daily lives. Work and family are at the center of our lives, the foundation of our dignity as a free people. When we deprive people of what they have earned, or take away their jobs, we destroy their dignity and undermine their families.

We cannot support our families unless there are jobs; and we cannot have jobs unless people have both money to invest and the faith to invest it. These are concepts that stem from an economic system that for more than 200 years has helped us master a continent, create a previously undreamed of prosperity for our people and has fed millions of others around the globe. That system will continue to serve us in the future if our government will stop ignoring the basic values on which it was built and stop betraying the trust and good will of the American workers who keep it going.

The American people are carrying the heaviest peacetime tax burden in our nation's history - - and it will grow even heavier, under present law, next January. We are taxing ourselves into economic exhaustion and stagnation, crushing our ability and incentive to save, invest and produce. This must stop. We must halt this fiscal self-destruction and restore sanity to our economic system. I have long advocated a 30 percent reduction in income tax rates over a period of three years. This phased tax reduction would begin with a 10 percent "down payment" tax cut in 1981, which the Republicans and Congress and I have already proposed.

A phased reduction of tax rates would go a long way toward easing the heavy burden on the American people. But we shouldn't stop here.

Within the context of economic conditions and appropriate budget priorities during each fiscal year of my Presidency, I would strive to go further. This would include improvement in business depreciation taxes so we can stimulate investment in order to get plants and equipment replaced, put more Americans back to work and put our nation back on the road to being competitive in world commerce. We will also work to reduce the cost of government as a percentage of our gross national product.

The first task of national leadership is to set honest and realistic priorities in our policies and our budget, and I pledge that my administration will do that. When I talk of tax cuts, I am reminded that every major tax cut in this century has strengthened the economy, generated renewed productivity and ended up yielding new revenues for the government by creating new investment, new jobs and more commerce among our people.

The present administration has been forced by the Republicans to play follow-the-leader with regard to a tax cut. But, in this election year we must take with the proverbial "grain of salt" any tax cut proposed by those who have given us the greatest tax increase in our history.

When those in leadership give us tax increases and tell us we must also do with less, have they thought about those who've always had less -- especially the minorities? This is like telling them that just as they step on the first rung of the ladder of opportunity, the ladder is being pulled out from under them. That may be the Democratic leadership's message to the minorities, but it won't be our message. Ours, ours will be: We have to move ahead, but we're not going to leave anyone behind.

Thanks to the economic policies of the Democratic Party, millions of Americans find themselves out of work. Millions more have never even had a fair chance to learn new skills, hold a decent job or secure for themselves and their families a share in the prosperity of this nation. It's time to put America back to work, to make our cities and towns resound with the confident voices of men and women of all races, nationalities and faiths bringing home to their families a decent paycheck they can cash for honest money. For those without skills, we'll find a way to help them get skills. For those without job opportunities, we'll stimulate new opportunities, particularly in the inner cities where they live. For those who have abandoned hope, we'll restore hope and we'll welcome them into a great national crusade to make America great again!

When we move from domestic affairs and cast our eyes abroad, we see an equally sorry chapter on the record of the present administration.

- A Soviet combat brigade trains in Cuba, just 90 miles from our shores.

- A Soviet army of invasion occupies Afghanistan, further threatening our vital interests in the Middle East.

- America's defense strength is at its lowest ebb in a generation, while the Soviet Union is vastly outspending us in both strategic and conventional arms.

- Our European allies, looking nervously at the growing menace from the East, turn to us for leadership and fail to find it.

- And, incredibly, more than 50 of our fellow Americans have been held captive for over eight months by a dictatorial foreign power that holds us up to ridicule before the world. Adversaries large and small test our will and seek to confound our resolve, but we are given weakness when we need strength; vacillation when the times demand firmness.

The Carter Administration lives in the world of make-believe. Every day, drawing up a response to that day's problems, troubles, regardless of what happened yesterday and what will happen tomorrow. But you and I live in a real world disasters are overtaking our nation without any real response from Washington. This is make-believe, self-deceit, and -- above all -- transparent hypocrisy. For example, Mr. Carter says he supports the volunteer army, but he lets military pay and benefits slip so low that many of our enlisted personnel are actually eligible for food stamps. Re-enlistment rates drop and, just recently, after he fought all week against a proposal to increase the pay of our men and women in uniform, he helicoptered to our carrier, the U.S.S. Nimitz, which was returning from long months of duty and told the crew that he advocated better pay for them and their comrades! Where does he really stand, now that he's back on shore?

Well, I'll tell you where I stand. I do not favor a peacetime draft or registration, but I do favor pay and benefit levels that will attract and keep highly motivated men and women in our volunteer forces and an active reserve trained and ready for an instant call in case of an emergency. You know, there may be a sailor at the helm of the ship of state, but the ship has no rudder. Critical decisions are made at times almost in comic fashion, but who can laugh? Who was not embarrassed when the administration handed a major propaganda victory in the United Nations to the enemies of Israel, our staunch Middle East ally for three decades, and then claim that the American vote was a "mistake," the result of a "failure of communication" between the President, his Secretary of State, and his U.N. Ambassador? Who does not feel a growing sense of unease as our allies, facing repeated instances of an amateurish and confused administration, reluctantly conclude that America is unwilling or unable to fulfill its obligations as the leader of the free world? Who does not feel rising alarm when the question in any discussion of foreign policy is no longer, "Should we do something?" but, "Do we have the capacity to do anything?"

The Administration which has brought us to this state is seeking your endorsement for four more years of weakness, indecision, mediocrity, and incompetence. No, No. Americans should vote until he or she has asked: Is the United States stronger and more respected now than it was three and a half years ago? Is the world safer, a safer place in which to live? It is the responsibility of the President of the United States, in working for peace, to ensure that the safety of our people cannot successfully be threatened by a hostile foreign power. As President, fulfilling that responsibility will be my No. 1 priority.

We are not a warlike people. Quite the opposite. We always seek to live in peace. We resort to force infrequently and with great reluctance -- and only after we have determined that it is absolutely necessary. We are awed -- and rightly so -- by the forces of destruction at loose in the world in this nuclear era. But neither can we be naive or foolish. Four times in my lifetime America has gone to war, bleeding the lives of its young men into the sands of beachheads, the fields of Europe and the jungles and rice paddies of Asia. We know only too well that war comes not when the forces of freedom are strong, it is when they are weak that tyrants are tempted. We simply cannot learn these lessons the hard way again without risking our destruction.

Of all the objectives we seek, first and foremost is the establishment of lasting world peace. We must always stand ready to negotiate in good faith, ready to pursue any reasonable avenue that holds forth the promise of lessening tensions and furthering the prospects of peace. But let our friends and those who may wish us ill take note: the United States has an obligation to its citizens and to the people of the world never to let those who would destroy freedom dictate the future course of human life on this planet. I would regard my election as proof that we have renewed our resolve to preserve world peace and freedom. This nation will once again be strong enough to do that.

This evening marks the last step, save one, of a campaign that has taken Nancy and me from one end of this great land to the other, over many months and thousands of miles.

There are those who question the way we choose a president; who say that our process imposes difficult and exhausting burdens on those who seek the office. I have not found it so. It is impossible to capture in words the splendor of this vast continent which God has granted as our portion of His creation. There are no words to express the extraordinary strength and character of this breed of people we call Americans. Everywhere we have met thousands of Democrats, Independents, and Republicans from all economic conditions and walks of life bound together in that community of shared values of family, work, neighborhood, peace and freedom. They are concerned, yes, they are not frightened. They are disturbed, but not dismayed. They are the kind of men and women Tom Paine had in mind when he wrote, during the darkest days of the American Revolution, "We have it in our power to begin the world over again." Nearly 150 years after Tom Paine wrote those words, an American president told the generation of the Great Depression that it had a "rendezvous with destiny." I believe that this generation of Americans today has a rendezvous with destiny.

Tonight, let us dedicate ourselves to renewing the American compact. I ask you not simply to "Trust me," but to trust your values -- our values -- and to hold me responsible for living up to them. I ask you to trust that American spirit which knows no ethnic, religious, social, political, regional or economic boundaries; the spirit that burned with zeal in the hearts of millions of immigrants from every corner of the Earth who came here in search of freedom.

Some say that spirit no longer exists. But I have seen it -- I have felt it -- all across the land, in the big cities, the small towns and in rural America. It is still there, ready to blaze into life if you and I will stimulate our economy, increase productivity and put America back to work. The time is now to limit Federal spending; to insist of a stable monetary reform and to free ourselves from imported oil. The time is now to resolve that the basis of a firm and principled foreign policy is one that takes the world as it is and seeks to change it by leadership and example, not by harangue, harassment or wishful thinking. The time is now to say that while we shall seek new friendships and expand and improve others, but we shall not do so by breaking our word or casting aside old friends and allies. And, the time is now to redeem promises once made to the American people, by another candidate, in another time and another place.

He said:

"For three long years I have been going up and down this country preaching that government -- Federal, state, and local -- costs too much. I shall not stop that preaching. As an immediate program of action, we must abolish useless offices. We must eliminate unnecessary functions of government.

"We must consolidate subdivisions of government and, like the private citizen, give up luxuries which we can no longer afford."

And then he said:

"I propose to you, my friends, and through you, that government of all kinds, big and little, be made solvent and that the example be set by the President of the United State and his Cabinet."

That was Franklin Delano Roosevelt's words as he accepted theDemocratic nomination for President in 1932.

The time is now, my fellow Americans, to recapture our destiny, to take it into our own hands. And to do this will take many of us, working together. I ask you tonight, all over this land, to volunteer your help in this cause so we can carry our message throughout the land.

Isn't it time that we, the people, carried out these unkept promises? That we pledge to each other and to all America on this July day 48 years later, that we now intend to do just that.

I have thought of something that is not part of my speech and I'm worried over whether I should do it. Can we doubt that only a Divine Providence placed this land, this island of freedom, here as a refuge for all those people in the world who yearn to breathe free? Jews and Christians enduring persecution behind the Iron Curtain; the boat people of Southeast Asia, Cuba, and Haiti; the victims of drought and famine in Africa, the freedom fighters of Afghanistan, and our own countrymen held in savage captivity.

I'll confess that I've been a little afraid to suggest what I'm going to suggest. I'm more afraid not to. Can we begin our crusade joined together in a moment of silent prayer?

God bless America.

Thank you.

Chapter 8: Using the Middle Ground Method of Argumentation

Introduction

In this final lesson of English 102, you will learn how to create a middle ground argument. Unlike the Toulmin and Rogerian methods where one side is argued over another, the middle ground argument mediates between two sides of an issue, finding a middle ground solution. In other words, this argumentative position seeks to forward a compromise or a mediated solution between two positions.

When individuals take a particular viewpoint or argue for a particular position on an issue, sometimes they may take an all or nothing approach to that issue. This is especially true of issues that have moral or religious implications. For instance, abortion and the issue of the death penalty are topics that tend to divide people into clear positions. However, most issues in life are generally not that divisive, and individuals are likely to hold viewpoints on these issues to which they are much less committed. With these issues, it might be possible and often makes sense to create a compromise position capable of persuading an audience. This is where learning how to take a middle approach to an issue can be valuable.

Taking a Middle Ground Position

Having established that the middle ground approach to an issue is a mediated position between two opposing sides, now we will consider several possible ways to craft such a compromise argument. One approach is to simply identify and confine one's argument to the common ground both sides might share. In this approach, you might find out the key claims or desires of each side and determine if there are any claims or desires that they have in common. It might be possible to simply agree to do or commit to only those items on which both sides agree. This approach is much less ambitious but can have a greater chance of achieving agreement. Another approach is a little more complicated but has the possibility of resulting in a more substantial agreement. This would include some form of bargaining. One might take equal parts of each argument, exchanging one for another, until something like a composite position with parts from each of the opposing sides is formed. Still another approach to achieving some form of middle ground agreement is to simply split the difference. That is, for instance, if one side wants the group to purchase 100 widgets and another side wants the group to get 50, it would make sense to settle on the mean number 75. This is different than bargaining because rather than exchanging concessions on particular points, one is proposing a mean or median of the two positions. This is often easiest to do when the point of disagreement has a value that can be averaged. For instance, we discussed the easy ability to average the number of widgets a group might purchase. It would be more difficult if the group were debating what color car to purchase. In this example it would not be possible to simply merge yellow and blue to settle on a green car. Colors are categories not values, so compromise in this case is trickier.

Another way to understand the middle ground approach is through illustration. Take a look at the following diagram:

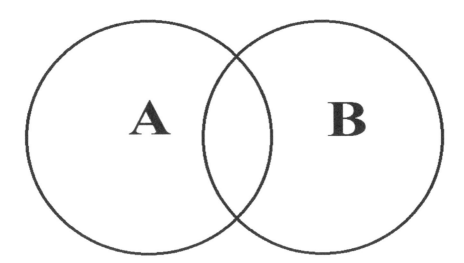

Figure 8.1: A Venn diagram shows two circles which slightly overlap in the middle. The one on the left is labeled "A," and the one on the right is labeled "B."

Let's say that this diagram illustrates the 'prayer in school' issue. People who are on the 'A' side believe that children should be allowed to express their religious beliefs in school. On the other hand, people on the 'B' side are against this idea – stating that this violates the United States constitution. As we discussed in lessons six and seven, in the Rogerian method of argumentation, 'A' would point out the counter argument, argue that side 'A' is correct, but then would show 'B' the common ground between both sides. For example, 'A' might tell 'B' that both hold common views on the United States First Amendment: "Congress shall make no law respecting an establishment of religion, or prohibiting the free exercise thereof." 'A' could state that this common ground proves the 'A' side - these children should be allowed the 'free exercise' of their religion by praying in schools.

Now, take a look at diagram below, illustrating the middle ground argument.

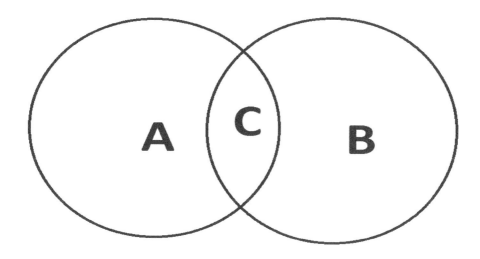

Figure 8.2: A Venn diagram shows two circles which slightly overlap in the middle. The one on the left is labeled "A," and the one on the right is labeled "B." The area of overlap in the middle is labeled "C."

Let's say that this diagram illustrates prayer in schools again. Again, 'A' is for prayer in schools and 'B' is against the proposition. The middle-ground solution, or 'C', would be the compromise for this issue. Unlike the Rogerian argument which uses an argument for the common ground as a means of convincing the other side of the error of their ways, the middle ground approach seeks to forge a genuine compromise between the two positions. For instance, an example of the 'C' position for the 'prayer in school' issue would be to allow students to have a moment of silence. During this time, the student can either choose to pray or sit quietly and do nothing. This way, the 'A' side can still express its beliefs, but 'B' can maintain its stance as well. Option 'C' would be the middle ground option.

Here's another example of a middle ground argument. Take a look at the below diagram, depicting the popular 'uniforms in school' argument.

A _____ **B** _____ **C**

Figure 8.3: A diagram shows a horizontal line labeled with three letters: "A" on the left, "B" in the center, and "C" on the right.

Some feel as though uniforms would help solve issues with gangs and bullying in school (let's say option 'A'). However, others believe that school uniforms could potentially stifle a student's individuality (option 'C'). A way to compromise – or meet in the middle – for this issue would be to allow students to choose their own clothing, but give these students limitations in what they are allowed to wear (restrict certain colors, immodest clothing, and various athletic sports teams). That would be option 'B.' This creates a compromise between these two positions, and this compromise allows the two extreme positions to meet in the middle.

In our own personal lives, we often have to learn how to compromise – whether it is at divvying up work duties on a team or deciding on what to order at a restaurant. Our lives are filled with compromises, and rarely are we able to fully choose one side completely over the other when a decision impacts more than just ourselves. Creating a compromise, or a middle ground argument, is often considered to be a balanced approach to argumentation.

When you form a middle ground essay, remember that this essay should still contain the same components as the other two arguments: a claim, modes of support, warrant, backing, and qualifiers. You should state this claim (or thesis) at the bottom of your opening paragraph. You can also decide what works best for your middle ground approach – claiming the common ground and/or compromising between two sides. Along with explaining your middle ground stance on an issue, you will also have to explain the two opposing sides. It is important to include the modes of support (ethos, pathos, and especially logos) with each section of this essay (each side and the middle ground section). If you have a section that does not contain research, you quite possibly could be creating a fallacy, known as the "Fallacy of Moderation." It is false to assume that the middle position is correct simply because it rests between two extreme positions. You must prove this middle position through research.

A HISTORICAL EXAMPLE OF A MIDDLE GROUND ARGUMENT: THE GREAT COMPROMISE OF 1787

The middle ground method of argumentation is not new. History is replete with examples of middle ground arguments emerging to reconcile the positions of opposing sides. This has been especially true in political history, where compromise and the fashioning of inventive middle ground solutions are often essential to stability. For example, in United States history, the middle ground solution was critical to the formation of our government, which emerged in 1787. Labeled by generations of history books as "The Great Compromise" or the "Connecticut Compromise" of the U.S. Constitutional Convention, it is worth reviewing the series of events as an important example of the power of this kind of argumentation.

First, you may recall that the country was deeply divided over how to proceed only a decade after the U.S. had declared independence in 1776. The new nation was operating under the Articles of Confederation, which was little more than a pledge of friendship among the various states. The central government under the Articles of Confederation was extremely weak, lacking the ability to raise sufficient revenue, engage in effective foreign and security policy, or even regulate trade between the various states. All of this made it extremely difficult to do business in the early American Republic. Merchants and the business community were particularly keen to see the Articles of Confederation strengthened to provide for a more coherent and stable economic base. Opposing this idea, however, were the many individuals and groups who saw the move to a stronger central government as a move back toward the kind of tyranny from a distant authority which they had so recently thrown off in the revolution. This belief was most prominent among the nation's many farmers and rural citizens who had less reason to support such things as increased interstate commerce. Consequently, when the state delegates met in Philadelphia in 1787, they were meeting to discuss how far it might be possible to go in strengthening the central government without alienating a large portion of the population who opposed such a move.

Moreover, this tension between rural and business America was not the only dividing line leading into the convention. The division between large states and small states was also important. Large states like Virginia and New York would benefit from a system in which states were represented in the central government according to their populations. Small states feared that this would result in large states making policies that were favorable to them at the expense of states with less population. Thus, states like Delaware and New Jersey argued that each state be represented equally in whatever form of central government eventually emerged.

The so called "Great Compromise" emerged in response to this latter conflict. The Virginia delegation arrived at the convention with a "Virginia Plan" that called for, among other things, a bicameral (two house) legislature, with allocation of seats in both houses determined by state population. Members of the first house would be elected by the citizens of their states and the members of the other house would be nominated by their state legislatures and approved by the first house. This would mean that states with large populations would have the lion's share of seats in the new government, a position that was countered by small states in the form of the alternate "New Jersey Plan." The New Jersey plan began by arguing that Virginia had no right to completely remake the Articles of Confederation. Delegates were only sent to Philadelphia to adjust them, not create an entirely new government. Consequently, the New Jersey plan argued for keeping the single house legislature that existed under the Articles and having membership in that house apportioned to give each state an equal vote. The two positions on how to apportion power in the new government were diametrically opposed, and the potential of a compromise was in doubt when the small states threatened to leave the convention.

To overcome this stalemate the issue was referred to a smaller committee consisting of only one delegate from each state. This committee essentially came back with a middle ground approach, taking parts of each plan and merging them into one (the composite or bargaining approach that was discussed earlier). From the Virginia Plan, two houses were proposed with the first house having seats apportioned according to the state's population. However, like the New Jersey Plan, the second house would have an equal number of representatives and votes from each state. A few additional adjustments to this basic compromise eventually resulted in the bicameral legislative framework the U.S. has today. Thus, the middle ground approach to reconciling the positions of Virginia and New Jersey carried the day. This was an approach that not only alleviated the small state–large state divide, it also created the added check and balance of two rather than one legislative organ, a result which served to assuage some of the fears of those who saw the new government as a potential tool for a future tyrant. Take a look at the below diagram which illustrates this historical event.

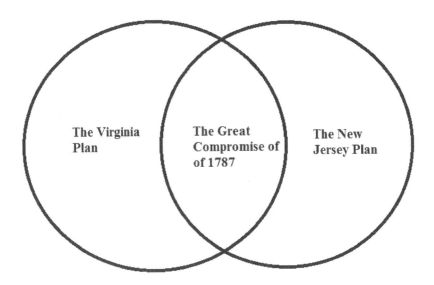

Figure: 8.4: Venn diagram shows two circles which slightly overlap in the middle. The one on the left is labeled "The Virginia Plan," and the one on the right is labeled "The New Jersey Plan." The area of overlap in the middle is labeled "The Great Compromise of 1787."

Now, take a look at the Table 8.1 below which demonstrates how a middle ground essay could be organized.

Table 8.1: How a Middle Ground Essay May be Organized

Issue at Stake	The state delegates who met in Philadelphia in 1787 were meeting to discuss how far it might be possible to go in strengthening the central government without alienating a large portion of the population who opposed such a move.
The Virginia Plan	Merchants and the business community thought a strong central government provided for a more coherent and stable economic base. Large states like Virginia and New York would benefit from a system in which states were represented in the central government according to their populations. This side advocated the "Virginia Plan" which meant that states with large populations would have the lion's share of seats in the new government

The New Jersey Plan	Many individuals and rural groups saw the move to a stronger central government as a move back toward the kind of tyranny from a distant authority which they had so recently thrown off in the revolution. Small states feared that a central government would result in large states making policies that were favorable to them at the expense of states with less population. This side advocated the "New Jersey Plan" which gave each state one vote.
Demonstrate the Middle Ground – The Compromise	From the Virginia Plan, two houses were proposed with the first house having seats apportioned according to the state's population. From the New Jersey Plan, the second house would have an equal number of representatives and votes from each state. This approach not only alleviated the small state – large state divide, it also created the added check and balance of two rather than one legislative organ, a result which served to assuage some of the fears of those who saw the new government as a potential tool for a future tyrant.

This is just one of the more famous examples of how middle ground arguments are an essential feature of democratic government. However, one need not go so far back in American history to find others. The next time you read or hear about the latest negotiation over some national or state legislative proposal, think about the middle ground approach and how it might ultimately serve to be the way by which the political contest is resolved.

FINAL NOTES FOR ENGLISH 102

Through this semester, you learned how to read works with a critical eye. You also learned the methods of support, recognized these methods in historical arguments, and utilized these methods in your own arguments. This course also showed you how to avoid argumentative fallacies in research and in your own writing. You also learned three methods of argumentation: the Toulmin, Rogerian, and middle ground. Finally, you learned the importance of utilizing strong, academic research in your writing, and how to best present your writing, using an organized, correctly-formatted work.

As you complete this course, consider all that you have learned this semester. At the beginning of this course, you examined your approach to writing. In this examination, you may have realized that your approach to writing needed a bit of help, whether your issue was procrastination, organization, or research. Perhaps you learned that your writing approach was actually quite strong, only needing fine tuning here and there. Now that you have completed this course, think about all that you have learned. If you were to complete this evaluation again, would your answers change?

In our everyday lives, whether it is work, school, or home, challenges and issues are presented to us. Often, we must learn how to 'fight' for our beliefs in these environments. You may not remember the terminology presented in this course in the future, but hopefully you took away one key point: to 'win' a persuasive argument, you must remember your audience. What will convince an audience? Convincing an audience takes strong writing, clear organization, solid evidence, and a fair presentation of the facts.

Congratulations! You have completed English 102.